Sticks and Stones

The Life and Times of a Journeyman Printer

Hertford, Dunstable, Cheltenham and Wolverton

Harry Edwards

The Book Castle

First published July 2001
By
The Book Castle
12 Church Street
Dunstable
Bedfordshire LU5 4RU

ISBN 1 903747 01 5

Typeset by the Author

Printed by Creative Print and Design Group
Saxon Way, Harmondsworth,Middx, UB7 0LW

Contents

Acknowledgments

My grateful thanks are due to Mr. Stanley Harrison for information regarding his research on the making of Arabic type; to Mr. Nigel Roche of the St. Brides Printing Library, and to Mr. Ron Walding and Mr. Dave Taylor of the William Clowes Print Museum at Beccles, for their unstinting help in allowing me to obtain some of the photographs used in this book; and to Gloria Isaacs for proofreading and offering useful advice. Also to a number of past colleagues who have helped to jog my memory over events long since passed.

My thanks also to Herts and Essex Newspapers and to the *Dunstable Gazette* for supplying or permitting the use of some of the photographs appearing in this book.

Chapter One

Still wet behind the ears

Christmas 1939 and my father came home on leave from the army. "You'll be fourteen in March" he said. "Have you thought about what you are going to do when you leave school?" "I want to be an electrician" I replied. I was very keen on electricity. We only had gas in the house but I had bought a switch, a bulb and bulb-holder with a small celluloid shade, a short length of insulated electric wire, and a battery, out of my pocket money, and had fitted up an electric light in my bedroom. "Printing's a good job" said Dad. "Some of them are earning five pounds a week. I've got a friend who works at a printer's. I'll ask him to come and talk to you." This short conversation was to shape my life for the next half-century.

Some time later Dad's friend Bert Gostling, known as "Gander", who was a reader at Stephen Austin & Sons Ltd., General and Oriental Printers, of Hertford, came to see me. I knew Bert by sight and reputation as he was the fast bowler for Hertingfordbury Cricket Club. He asked me to read a passage from a book and then said he would try to get me an interview with the works manager. In due course my mother received a letter from Mr. Skerman, the works manager, asking her to take me to an interview. We attended at the appropriate time and once again I was asked to read aloud a very long passage, this time from a book containing very long paragraphs. Mr. Skerman was obviously satisfied and I was asked to report for work on 1st April, 1940. This seemed to be an ominous date being All Fools Day, and in the event my brother went down with German measles so it was suggested that I postpone my starting date until 8th April. In the meantime I could earn a few shillings by tidying up the works manager's garden.

This was good in some respects as it allowed me to get to know Mr. Skerman a little better away from the work environment. The work involved only two hours in the mornings

1

and two in the afternoons and consisted mainly of tidying up the garden in general and a little hand weeding, etc., with long breaks for tea and home-made cake in between provided by Mrs. Skerman, who thought that a young boy should not work too hard!

Before I started work I had to sign my indentures. In my village there existed the Walter Wallinger Charity which was "for putting out Children, the Sons and Daughters of the Housekeepers of the Parish of Hertingfordbury, in the County of Hertford, Apprentices". This was founded at a time when employers had to be paid to apprentice children to learn a trade. At the time I started work it usually helped, for example, boys who were to become carpenters to buy their tools. In my case the trustees paid my employer £25 to instruct me in the "Art, Trade, and Business of Printing" and pay "in lieu of good and sufficient meat, drink, and lodging the following weekly wages, namely, thirteen shillings and sixpence in the first year" and specified weekly wages for the following six years, this being a seven-year apprenticeship. I also had to sign that "during which time the said Apprentice agrees that his Masters faithfully shall serve, their secrets keep, and their lawful commands everywhere gladly do and obey, he shall do no hurt to his said Masters, nor wilfully suffer it to be done by others, but the same to the best of his power shall hinder or forthwith give Notice to his said Masters, he shall not waste the goods of his said Masters, nor lend them unlawfully to any person, shall not contract matrimony, nor at any time depart or absent himself from his said Masters' service without their leave, but in all things as a good and faithful Apprentice shall demean and behave himself towards his said Masters and all theirs during the said term".

This awesome-sounding contract was signed in the presence of my father, whose regiment was fortunately stationed near-by, two directors of the company, and three trustees of the Walter Wallinger Charity. The signed indentures were lodged with a local firm of solicitors and a report of my progress had to be sent to them on a regular basis to ensure that the company was giving me the correct training.

On 8th April, with shoes well polished and with hair neatly parted, I set off on my bicycle to Hertford. When I came to the hill out of the village I didn't have the strength to push the pedals and went back home. My mother thought I was suffering from nerves and suggested that I had another cup of tea and try again. Then she suddenly came over to where I was sitting. "Open your shirt" she said. There, on the base of my neck and chest were the red measles spots. So my eventual date for commencing work was 22nd April.

So, on Monday 22nd April, sharp at 8 o'clock, a very nervous young lad presented himself at the works manager's office. After showing me round the factory he took me to the reading room where all apprentices spent their first few months reading copy to the readers, running errands, and generally learning where everything was and who everybody was, as well as the meanings of the various marks used in proof reading. I was known as a "copy holder" and assigned to Dad's friend Bert.

The reading room was light and airy with two large double-sided desks in the body of the room and a small one in the corner. At our desk I sat next to Bert Gostling and next to him sat Bert Bentley with his copy holder Sheila Bunn. Opposite us were Bob Claydon and his copy holder Joan Wilson, a lovely young woman who was very kind to me in my early days. Next to him was Noel Wilkinson, who read mostly Arabic proofs. At the corner desk Sid Skerman, the works manager's brother, read all of the other oriental language proofs, Chinese, Tamil, Burmese, etc. Behind us, at the other desk, sat Evelyn Walls, the young woman who was responsible for the des-patching of galley proofs and page proofs to customers, and who was known affectionately as "Toddles". Opposite her was Bill Butler, a rather saturnine man known as "The General", who was foreman of the department.

Finding my way round the factory was like exploring a whole new world and the terms and expressions used were completely alien to me. The factory comprised a three-storey building with a basement on one side of a yard with a newer, two-storey building on the far side which housed the machine room and the bindery. The printing industry has its origins in the church and a group of men working together in a printing shop were called a "companionship", which had over the years been abbreviated to "ship". On the third floor of the main building were the magazine ship, which produced magazines, and the oriental ship, which dealt with all oriental work, mainly composed by hand. The second floor housed the book ship, the Monotype keyboards and casters and a large proofing press, capable of producing high-quality colour proofs. The jobbing ship, which dealt with letter headings, business cards, advertisements, and things of that nature occupied the first floor, together with the Mercury ship, which was responsible for the printing of the *Hertfordshire Mercury*, the local news-paper, a large hand-operated proofing press, and the works manager's office. In the corner in a partitioned-off section were two Linotype machines. On the ground floor was the front office, including the Mercury office, rooms for the reporters, sub-editors, etc. and a metal foundry. The basement housed a few small printing machines and the giant Cossor, which printed the *Mercury* once a week.

Shortly after I started work I was approached by the Father of the Chapel, or F.O.C. as he was known, to join the union, which in those days was the Typographical Association. This was a precondition to working in the printing industry which was considered by many to be a hotbed of socialism. As previously mentioned, printing had its origins in the church, and the in-house union organisation was known as a "chapel", hence the title "Father of the Chapel". In due course I was issued with a membership card and a badge, which I proudly wore in the lapel of my jacket.

My first pay packet was a major event. There was a passage-way leading to the front door of the factory building in which stood the two time clocks where we "clocked" in and out every time we entered or left the factory and beside these was a small hatchway, the other side of which was the front office. Every Friday lunchtime we queued along this passage-way to hand in our clock cards and receive our pay packets from one of the office staff. My pay for the first year of my apprenticeship was thirteen shillings and sixpence a week, less fourpence deduc-tions for National Insurance. I gave my mother ten shillings of this which left me with the princely sum of three shillings and twopence for the week. However, with careful management, this enabled me to go to the cinema once, or twice if I sat in the one-and-sixpennys, and still have a few pence left over with which to buy sweets, especially if I walked both ways.

There were three cinemas in Hertford then—the County, the Castle, and the Regent. The newest of these and by far the best was the County Cinema, with marble stairs leading to the balcony seats and a very select tea room with a goldfish pool illuminated by soft lights set into the wall. Next in line came the Castle Cinema which had neither a tearoom nor a balcony but was nevertheless a good cinema. Finally there was the Regent Cinema, known locally as the "bug and flea pit". This was a small cinema with low-priced seats but it occasionally showed a good film. Sadly this cinema was closed down as a fire hazard after an electric fire was discovered on a window ledge adjacent to a curtain which was waving gently in a draught.

Seat prices ranged from one shilling and threepence to three shillings and sixpence. The one and threes, as they were known, were right at the front and so I usually elected to sit in the one and sixes. This enabled me to go twice to the cinema provided I walked there and back or once if I decided to buy some fish and chips from Hugget's fish and chip shop on the way home. It was a really good end to the day, walking home in the dark and eating piping hot fish and chips straight from its newspaper wrapping.

The County Cinema was about two miles from where I lived and as I had always been used to walking this was no hardship. I made it a personal test to see how quickly I could walk the two miles and eventually managed to cover the distance in twenty minutes.

One of the things which Bert asked my father when he knew I had the job was "Does your boy swear?" "I haven't heard him" replied Dad. "Well, he soon will" said Bert. I had been working only a few days when Bert sent me with a proof to one of the compositors with a message to do something or other. "Mr. Gostling said 'will you do so and so'?" I told him. "Tell him he's a blankety-blankety-blank" was the reply. "I can't tell him that" I thought. I was soon to learn that the use of colourful adjectival phrases was the norm for the factory floor.

After my first week or two in the reading room I began to find my way around and lose some of my shyness. The atmosphere of the room was very friendly and a lot of good-natured banter went on between the men. The two Berts would get into a low-voiced conversation about where the girls had been the previous evening, who they'd been with, what they'd been doing, etc. A particular target was Evelyn. There were continuous references to "Toddles" with many a sly sideways glance to see if she was listening. Suddenly, without warning, Eve would turn round and plunge a pin into their backsides. There followed a dramatic display of pain and suffering, with Bob and Noel grinning away on the other side of the desk. Although they knew what to expect they did this on a regular basis, always with the same outcome. Occasionally they'd involve me by saying "What do you think boy?" Whatever I thought didn't matter as I, too, would then be on the receiving end of the pin. Although it was only the tip of the pin it hurt for some time afterwards.

Some soldiers had been billeted at the public house whose yard backed on to our factory and when they weren't copy-holding the girls would stroll over to the window and wave to them to the disapproval of "The General". He was quite a sombre man who didn't smile much and when he was present the room was fairly quiet. However, the moment he went out for any reason "Gander", who wasn't known for his quiet demeanour, would shout "the General's gorn" and everyone would lean back and relax and pass the snuff box round.

A chore that fell to the junior apprentice was to fetch snuff for the men. This involved calling at the tobacconist's shop on the way home to dinner and I can still recall the fragrant spicy smell as the fresh snuff was spooned into little quarter ounce packets. Most imbibers ordered only a quarter of an ounce at a time as this meant that it didn't have time to go stale but there was one heavy snuff taker who always ordered half an ounce. Smoking was not allowed in the workplace and many men took snuff, not only as a social habit but to prevent lead poisoning. In the early days of printing all type was hand set from lead type and the type cases had quite large accumulations of lead dust which could easily have been breathed in.

There was quite a ceremony with snuff taking. The box was passed around from hand to hand and, before taking a pinch of snuff, a man would first give his nose a good blowing. This was said to remove any lead dust that had settled in his nostrils. He would then rub the tips of his forefinger and thumb on his lapel or the edge of his apron and then tap the box lid before opening it and taking a pinch of snuff, giving a quick sniff into each nostril before closing the box and passing it on to the next man. A quick dusting with a handkerchief under the nose completed the operation.

There were differing ways of taking snuff. Some would take it as described above, others would take two pinches, one for each nostril, and others poured a small trail on to the back of their hand and ran their nose along, sniffing as they went. One man, who always ordered a half ounce at a time, used his thumb and first two fingers to take a huge pinch.

One of our customers was Haileybury College, a prestigious college which was attended only by the sons of the very wealthy, and whose magazine we printed. Every so often a group of the pupils, usually the younger ones, were brought on a tour of the works. On one such occasion one of the men was taking a pinch of snuff. "What are you doing?" asked one of the boys in a very refined voice. "I'm taking a pinch of snuff" replied the man. "Why?" said the boy. "To keep me awake" was the reply. "I'd like to try it" said the boy. So the man held out his snuff box and showed the boy how to take a pinch. The lad took a pinch and sniffed. Immediately tears sprang to his eyes and he went into a violent fit of sneezing and coughing. "Oh bugger!" he gasped.

Another incident involving snuff occurred in the machine room. A particular man was noted for always taking a pinch from somebody else's box but he seldom bought any of his own. One man decided to teach him a lesson. He bought a packet of electric snuff from a joke shop and kept pretending to take a pinch. "Give us a pinch Harry" said the man in question. "No, you wouldn't like this" replied Harry. "It's not the usual kind." However, the man persisted and in the end Harry offered him the box. The man took a huge pinch as usual and sniffed it into both nostrils. Suddenly his face turned purple and it looked as if his head would explode. He coughed and spluttered and rushed to the nearest tap to wash his nose and streaming eyes. Whether or not he learned his lesson is not certain but he was very wary of asking for other people's snuff for a very long time.

Some time during that Spring we had the first daylight air raid of the war. It was a lovely day with clear blue sky and we suddenly heard an unusual noise from outside. It sounded like lots of typewriters clattering away. We went to the window and, high in the sky, formations of bombers were flying over with tiny silver fighter 'planes weaving in and out between them. The noise was, of course, machine-gun fire. Desperate battles were being fought high above us yet it all seemed so remote. Eve climbed on to the desk to get a better look when suddenly the siren sounded. She was so surprised that she fell backwards off the desk and landed bottom first in a waste-paper basket.

It was decided that in future, as soon as the sirens sounded, everybody should go to the air raid shelters which were about five minutes away in the grounds of Hertford Castle. At first it was all taken quite seriously and everyone sat and talked and smoked or played cards until the all clear sounded. After a while, however, boredom set in and things were devised to pass the time. Tape measures were brought along and were used to find out which girl had the longest hair, or the biggest calves, or the tiniest waist, and which man had the largest biceps, etc. Eventually it got to the stage where we decided that it was perfectly safe above ground if nothing was happening in the area and we strolled around in the fresh air or just sat on the benches in the sunshine. At times like this, inside the great flintstone walls of the castle grounds, with its beautiful flower beds and almond trees, and the river running between green lawns, the war seemed far away.

This state of affairs could not continue indefinitely as work was suffering so it was decided that we should stay at work when the siren sounded but one of the men would be stationed on the roof and at the sound of approaching aircraft he would give warning and everyone would make for the safety of the stairs away from any flying glass. The possibility of a direct hit on the factory was no more than that of one on the air raid shelter.

After about three months in the reading room I was sent to work on the book ship, which is where my education really began.

Photo courtesy of Herts and Essex Newspapers

The Mercury Office in 1954

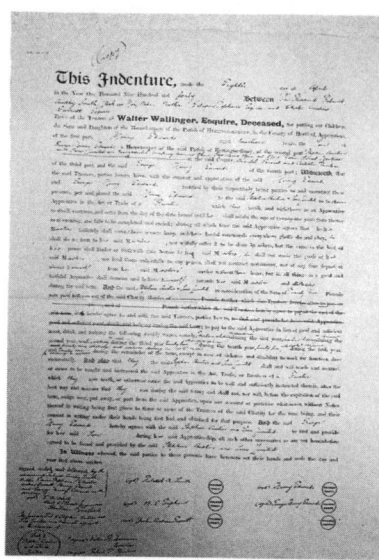

My Indentures

The Mercury Office today

My mother, father, me, and my brother John

Chapter Two

I become a printer's devil

I reported for work to the foreman of the book ship wearing my brand new white apron with a pocket at the front. The apron was too long for me and had to be folded over at the waist. It's a mystery why printers wore white aprons for such a dirty job but that was the standard at the time. Later, men wore a more sensible overall.

The book ship took up most of the second floor of the factory, with the Monotype casting room at one end and a press room and the Monotype keyboard department at the side. A door on the other side led to a small room where the estimators worked.

My foreman was Stanley Martin, a tall, red-haired, friendly man. He showed me round, introduced me to the men, and generally told me where everything was. Getting the men's names right took a few days, especially as they often used nicknames which I, as an apprentice, could not do. This was particularly confusing as there was a Joe Huckle and a Cecil Sams who was known as "Hickle". Most of the nicknames were friendly ones and used to people's faces, but a few were not. In addition to the ones already mentioned there were Gunner, Weasel, Gandy, Bunter, Chooka, Weeny, Granny, Horace, Hoppy, Bladder, Chanker, Haricot, Spider, Poofy, Chinger, and Chang.

The first thing I had to do was to learn the layout of the type case and this was achieved by "dissing", the word commonly used for distributing the type back

A double case

into the case. This was a tedious but necessary job and the advent of a new apprentice on the ship released the men for more productive work. There were basically two kinds of type:

type made at typefounders which was expensive to buy but which was very durable, and type cast within the factory which was cheap to produce and could be melted down and the metal used for casting new type. Only the founder's types and the larger types of the kind used for headlines were distributed. The case was designed so that the most commonly-used letters were in the centre of the case and in larger compartments than the rest. The letter "e", being the most used letter of the English alphabet, occupied the centre position and had a larger compartment than the other characters.

I now had to learn a whole new language concerning printing terminology. Each kind of type was known as a fount, pronounced font, and in fact today, probably because of American influences, is spelt as font in most applications and particularly in its use with computers. Each founder's fount was distinguished by a combination of grooves, called "nicks" on the front edge of the piece of type and this was a useful aid in recognising some of the more obscure type faces, especially ones of similar appearance. Monotype, the type which was cast within the factory, on the other hand, had one nick on the front and a very thin raised line on the back. This was to ensure that the type held together and that spaces didn't rise up making a black mark on the printed page.

Composing stick

Type was composed, or "set up", in a composing stick, a small adjustable hand-held tray which was set to the width of the page or column being composed. The type was set upside down, or "nicks up", from the left-hand side of the stick in order that it would appear the right way round when printed and one quickly learned to read type this way. When the stick was full the type was transferred to a "galley", which was a long metal tray, and when this was full a piece of wood or metal of the correct width, known as "furniture", was placed at the end, a long, tapering piece of wood called a "sidestick" was then placed down the side of the type and held in position by

A slip galley

12

wooden wedges known as "quoins". The galley was then taken to a small hand-operated press, ink rolled over the type, a length of paper called a galley slip placed over it, and the printing roller pulled over to make a galley proof or "pull". This then went to the reading department for proof-reading, together with the original copy.

After the type had been corrected it was made up into pages and then placed on a steel-topped table called a "stone", so-called because in the early days of printing they were in fact made of stone. The pages were then spaced out with furniture, a steel frame called a "chase" placed round them, and held in position by flat steel sidesticks called "steels" and expanding metal quoins which were tightened by means of a key. The whole thing was then known as a "forme" (*right*).

Everyone was kind to me, the new boy, and I felt things were going well. One day I was lifting a case of type, which was very heavy, on to a frame, when the case caught the corner of the frame, shooting the contents on to the floor. Stanley went a bright red and after hurling abuse at me told me to pick it all up and put the type back into its respective compartments. I must have looked very frightened as being shouted at by a foreman was a new experience for me. One of the men sidled up to me and said "Don't worry when Stan goes red. It's when he goes white that he's angry."

Once I was busy dissing when some of the men gathered round one of the "frames", the compositor's workplace, a sort of high desk with a sloping top on which the cases of type and galleys being worked on were placed, and began to talk excitedly. I heard things like "Come and look at this" and "I haven't seen one of those for a long time." Naturally I was curious and kept looking in their direction. "Come and look at this boy. We've got a type spider." I went over and on the frame was a galley with two pages of type on it and some

water. This was not unusual for water was sometimes sprinkled on the type to hold it together. "I can't see anything" I said. "Look, right there in the corner" said one. I craned my head over to see and suddenly the two pages were slammed together and I received a jet of water full in the face. It was the first but not the last time I was caught out and was all part of the learning process.

Another favourite trick was for the men to gather round and one of them to place a funnel in his belt and balance a shilling on his forehead and then tip his head forward and drop the shilling into the funnel. An apprentice would then be invited to try with the promise that if he could catch the shilling in the funnel he could keep it. Most boys fell for it and when their head was tilted back someone would tip a cupful of water into the funnel. I gradually got to know the other apprentices but as they had all been through the various indignities inflicted upon new boys they kept all the surprises to themselves.

By far the worst of these, however, was the use of the sidestick. Somebody would sneak up behind you, insert a sidestick between your legs, and start turning it. The trousers quickly started to twist round the stick followed by the skin on the inside of the thighs. It was a very painful and unforgettable experience. One man used to boast that he could turn over an elephant by this method. Needless to say this was only done to young lads.

I was very innocent when I started work but this was to change very rapidly. To relieve the chore of dissing and, so they said, to teach me to compose type, the men gave me rude poems to set up with the instruction that if any of the managers appeared I was to hide them and carry on dissing. It was certainly a useful exercise because they treated them as real jobs, reading them for errors, which I had to correct, and then get good clean proofs from the press.

One of my early jobs was to clean the proofing press *(below)* every morning. This involved pouring white spirit over the ink slab and hand roller to dissolve the previous day's ink and then wipe it clean with a coarse cloth called a "wiper". This done, fresh ink had to be applied to the roller with a palette knife and then worked backwards and forwards on the ink slab until it was covered in a smooth film. No protective gloves were provided and it was a dirty job which entailed washing one's hands in white spirit when it was finished followed by  several scrubbings with hot water and soap. People used to say that print was in their blood. It probably worked its way in over the years through the skin!

As we printed a lot of government work I was privileged, even at that age, to see some things which the general public did not see. I remember one particular book, produced for propaganda purposes, entitled *Belgium Unvanquished* which contained horrifying pictures of the devastation caused by the bombing of Antwerp. A regular job was a magazine entitled *La France*, which was produced for the Free French Forces. Although I could not speak a word of French, and still can't for that matter, I nevertheless learned to understand quite a bit so far as reading was concerned.

After I had been at work for a few months and had found my feet I was told that I had to go to work early on Friday mornings to help with the printing of the *Hertfordshire Mercury*. There were only a few people involved in this operation: two machine minders to run the printing machine, the maintenance man whose job it was to watch the machine for paper breaks, two packers, and the four most junior apprentices. We had to start work at 5.30 a.m. and the first boy in grabbed the hand truck. His job was to take the papers up in the lift to the ground floor and stack them in order ready for the delivery vans. The next two boys picked up the knives which meant that they would be helping the packers. The unfortunate boy who was last in had to take the papers off the machine as they were delivered in tens on a moving belt, which meant that he was stuck there until the end of the run, usually about half-past nine if there were no problems.

After we had finished printing we had half an hour off before we continued with the normal working day. Now, a couple of streets away was Wren's the bakers, and Friday morning was the day they made doughnuts, which were sold at a penny each or seven for sixpence. These doughnuts were hot, crisp and sugary, and bursting with jam, having just come from the boiling oil. Frequently I was asked by some of the men to bring back doughnuts for them so if they ordered, say, twelve between them that meant two free doughnuts for me. I can remember on one occasion eating seven hot doughnuts for lunch. I dread to think of the effect this would have on my digestive system now.

It was the practise then to have "lunch", or a mid-morning snack, at about half past ten or eleven o'clock. People would bring out a large piece of cake or a sandwich, held in a piece of paper to keep it clean, and perhaps have a cup of tea from a thermos flask. My favourite at that time was a piece of cold bread pudding. My mother made superb bread puddings, smooth and crisp underneath and crunchy on top and simply bursting with sultanas and currants. My criterion for a perfect bread pudding was that it could be held between thumb and finger tip and waved gently without breaking. I still drool when I think of the satisfying feel of the weight of it and the cool juicy taste as it passed over the teeth and tongue, and seldom bypass an opportunity to partake of a piece.

There was a spin-off to the job of stacking the bundles of papers. After the van drivers had finished delivering the *Mercurys* one of them had to go to London to make deliveries of commercial work. As it was wartime manpower was in short supply and frequently the boy who had done the stacking was asked to go as driver's mate. This was a great day out if not without its hazards but by the time I managed to get to that coveted position the daylight raids had virtually finished over London and although we often had to make diversions because of the devastation of the previous night's bombing, it was just one big adventure.

One of the van drivers, Alf, was a Londoner, and it was a wonderful experience to be driven round London by him. He had a great time swearing at taxi drivers and getting into heated conversations at the transport cafés where we had lunch. Those transport cafés in wartime Britain provided a wonderful service with their huge mugs of steaming tea or cocoa and good wholesome doorstep sandwiches.

Charlie Westwood, the maintenance man, was a great character although at times he had a short fuse. His job on Friday mornings, after helping to thread the web of paper in the machine, was to watch for tears in the paper and to stop the machine immediately he spotted one. This was a mesmeric task with the printed paper passing before his eyes in time with the beat of the machine and sometimes we would see his head gradually begin to drop until his chin touched his chest when he would sit up with a start. One day we stood behind one of the pillars in the basement and whistled short sharp notes in time with the rhythm of the machine. Charlie got up with a puzzled look on his face and oiled almost every part of the machine until he spotted us laughing. With that he grabbed a length of half-inch rope and chased us all round the machine room till he was breathless but, being Charlie, the incident was forgotten almost immediately.

The paper reels occasionally broke, causing a delay while the torn pieces were peeled off the rollers and the reel fed through again. One Good Friday I had arranged to meet my pals at about 10.30 a.m. knowing that we usually finished printing about 9.30 a.m. That day, however, everything went wrong. It was a particularly bad batch of paper and it kept breaking. Newsagents were 'phoning in to ask where their papers had got to, tempers were getting frayed, and the advertising manager came in to find out what the problem was. To ease the tension he sent out for lunch for us all and urged us to do our best. We persevered and eventually finished printing at about 1.30 p.m.

Dad had been invalided out of the army in 1941 and one Friday morning in winter he'd got up to see me off to work. There was an air raid in progress at the time and every ten minutes a German bomber would drone over, unmistakable by the sound of its unsynchronised engines, followed almost immediately by anti-aircraft fire, then another period of comparative quiet. It took me about ten minutes to cycle to work, so

Dad reckoned that if I left home as soon as the firing stopped it would just give me time to get there before another 'plane came over, the danger being, of course, from flying shrapnel. This I did, passing a silent anti-aircraft gun parked on a piece of open ground on the way. I opened the heavy door at the works entrance and took my bicycle through to the yard at the back. All was silent except for a shaft of yellow light emanating from the basement steps. I went down and the only person there was old Charlie, busy oiling the machine. "What are you doing here?" he asked. I must have looked surprised because it was Friday morning and I should have been there. "Look at the time" he said. I looked—and the hands of the clock were at twenty minutes past four. It transpired that the hour hand of our clock on the mantelpiece at home had worked loose and had slipped forward—and the clock was ten minutes fast to boot. I made myself comfortable on a couple of reels of paper and dozed for the next hour.

A task on which I spent hours in my early days was dropping, tying and packing pages. "Dropping" meant unlocking the metal chases and putting the furniture into racks according to size. The pages of type then had to be tied using a length of string called a "page cord". With only a strip of lead at the top and bottom of each page, approximately fifteen hundred individual pieces of type were tied so that it was possible to lift the whole page without a single piece dropping out. Having tied the pages they then had to be wrapped individually in sheets of paper with the job title and page number written on the ends and tops. These were then stored away in case of a reprint at a later date.

One compositor was known as "the lasso comp" because he seldom made a good job of tying which often resulted in a page being "pied", the term used when type was knocked over or disarranged. It then fell upon me to put the damaged page on to a galley, sprinkle some water over it to help it to stick together, and then make the page good before retying and packing it.

During my time on the book ship an incident occurred which caused me to lose my temper for one of the very few times in my life. There was a pressman who delighted in bullying apprentices in various ways. For example, he hung one apprentice on a coat hook by his jacket collar. One day I was working at the stone with one of the men, trying to learn the intricacies of imposition, and the pressman kept coming up behind me and flicking my ears, which was not only annoying but it also hurt. I told him to stop but he took no notice and continued pestering me. Suddenly something inside me snapped. I turned and hit him in the solar plexus with all my strength. He collapsed in a heap on the floor, writhing in pain. As the pain began to subside he started swearing at me and threatening to kill me. He staggered to his feet and picked up a piece of wood. At this point Stan the foreman stepped in. "You've been asking for that Joe," he said. "Now pack it up and get on with your work." Joe went off and eventually calmed down, but he never bothered me again. It was a valuable lesson to me in facing up to bullies.

After a few months on the book ship it was time to learn another aspect of the trade, this time jobbing printing.

Some tools used by the compositor

Planer

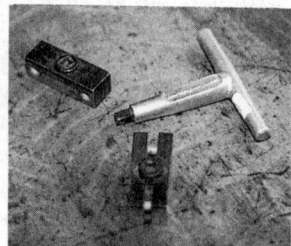

Mallet and shooting
stick

Metal quoins and
quoin key

Mitre

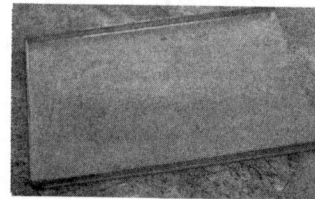

Quarto galley

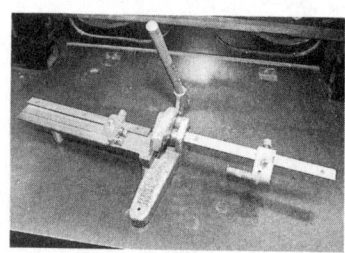

Lead and rule cutter

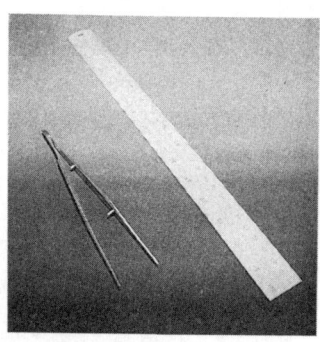

Typescale and tweezers

Chapter Three

Introduction to keyboard operating

The jobbing ship was on the first floor, together with the Mercury ship, a small room with two Linotype machines, a small press room, and the works manager's office. The foreman was Charlie Batchelor, a rather quiet man, and the men working on the ship were Bert Ince, the father of the chapel, Harry Cutts, and Fred Waller, all well over call-up age. The work here consisted mainly, as the word "jobbing" suggests, of a variety of work of a small nature, such as letter headings, advertisements, bills, packing leaflets, etc. One customer for whom we produced packing leaflets was a company called British Drug Houses and the type face used for the name of the drug,

A Linotype machine

which was the headline of the leaflet, was called Basuto. This was an exceptionally bold type with the hole in the middle of letters such as o, p, d, etc., being an oval offset to the right, but the customer insisted that in the case of the letter o the oval should slope to the left. It was just an idiosyncrasy on their part and as the body of the letter was square it was a simple matter to turn it through ninety degrees.

Jobbing printing, although usually associated with small printing shops, had its place at Stephen Austin's and was a useful experience, as I learnt how to lay out advertisements, using different sizes and weights of type to emphasize the important parts and to link them together in a positive but unobtrusive manner.

There was another apprentice of my age on the ship, Bob Smith, and two senior apprentices, Dennis Hipgrave on the Mercury Ship, and Cliff Andrews in the Linotype department. This was a potentially explosive situation and on a number of occasions we were caught talking when we should have been working and threats were made to separate us by sending us to different parts of the factory.

Most of the excitement, however, came from the various happenings connected with the Mercury Ship. Albert Murkin, the foreman, was a small, fiery-tempered man, and would frequently get into arguments, especially with George "Sonny" Mansfield, the reader of the *Mercury*. His job was to read not only for typographical errors but also to point out things like positional errors and maybe suggest alterations to the layout of adverts, etc. Occasionally Sonny, who was by nature a very quiet and friendly man, would come down and point out some alteration he thought needed doing. Suddenly Albert would erupt and let fly with a string of invectives. Voices would be raised and threats made to take one or the other into the office to see the manager. Many was the time that they arrived outside the office door but not once to my knowledge did they ever go in.

At one side of the room was a goods lift which went from the basement to the third floor. By the side of the lift was a bell push and a speaking tube so that if someone sent something up from, say, the basement they pressed the bell for the requisite floor and someone would speak down the voice tube and then place their ear to the mouthpiece to hear what the other person had to say. One day one of the men put some printing ink round the mouthpiece and then rang the bell. "It's for you Albert" he called. Albert went over and put his mouth to the tube and shouted "Yes?" and then placed his ear on the spot. Nobody answered so he went away muttering, with a ring of ink round his mouth and another round his ear.

Such was the richness of life on the Mercury ship. Some time later I had a short spell working there and found newspaper work far from my liking. It was the same thing week after week with Monday being devoted to the dissing of the previous week's paper, saving headlines and advertisements which would be used again, and generally getting black printing ink on hands, arms and apron. Tuesday would be fairly quiet, things would begin to speed up on Wednesday, while Thursday would be quite a frantic day trying to fit in all the last-minute items ready for Friday's printing.

There followed a slightly longer spell on the magazine ship, learning all about the intricacies of making up pages of type in two, three or four columns, and inserting pictures in the form of copper-faced blocks into place. This work was very interesting and probably formed the base from which I worked many years later managing origination departments. Finished pages were placed on galleys and stored in racks which were either down the side of the printing frames at which we worked or in large cabinets at the side of the room and these were labelled A, B, C, with numbers ranging from 1 to however many the rack would hold. Thus, if a galley proof was numbered D7 you knew the type was in rack D, shelf 7. However, one rack intrigued me. It was a metal rack which was screwed to the wall and labelled BN. There didn't seem to be any logic behind this so I asked one of the men why it had this unusual lettering. It transpired that one of the men was continually catching his shoulder on the rack as he passed and one day he said "that rack is a bloody nuisance" and from that day it became known as BN rack.

The foreman was Jack Boughton, a strict man but a good instructor and whose twinkling blue eyes behind steel-rimmed glasses showed a good sense of humour. There was also George, one of the oldest men in the factory, a tall man with long legs who used to walk home to lunch every day. He was a very fast walker and even when he was near retirement age few could keep up with him.

At the age of 16 I joined the Civil Defence, or the A.R.P. as it was then known. What brilliant Whitehall mind had the inventiveness to call a body of people, who were there to deal with incidents, Air Raid Precautions? I applied to Sir Henry Richards, who was head warden at Hertingfordbury, to become a messenger. However, Sir Henry said that there was no real need for a messenger in the village and that I should become an air raid warden. Having been given my identity papers I went to the stores at Hertford and collected my navy blue battledress, beret, boots, gaiters, steel helmet and civilian duty respirator, together with a large silver badge. From this time on my days were fully occupied with working in the daytime and taking my turn of duty at night. There were also courses to attend in the evenings, which included first aid, rescue, and fire fighting, in addition to instruction on pro-cedural matters. The wardens' post was the study at Sir Henry's house, Dell Cottage. When the sirens sounded the alert those on duty made their way quickly to the post. It was quite an eerie place in the middle of the night. First there was the door to go through, followed by wooden shutters, and then a heavy velvet blackout curtain. Having got inside and made sure that the room was lightproof, one made one's way gingerly across the room in pitch darkness, switched on the light and signed in. There was a set of bells on the wall of the study and occasionally these bells would tinkle away as a mouse got inside the wiring system somewhere along the line. We would first of all patrol the village to ensure that no lights were showing and then return to the post till the all clear sounded, unless of course any incident occurred.

I got into the habit of placing my clothes in the strict order of dressing on a chair beside my bed so that I could get up in the dark and dress with the minimum of time and effort. One such night when it was my turn on duty the sirens sounded. I jumped out of bed, quickly dressed, and hurried along the road to the wardens' post. Still not fully awake, I passed beneath the overhanging branches of a yew tree. At that precise moment an owl hooted from the tree and I nearly jumped out of my skin.

The nights when I was off duty I usually slept through the air raids, which was just as well as I still had to go to work the next day, but like millions of others at that time I discovered just how little sleep one can manage with if really put to it.

Some time during my third year it was decided that I should learn to operate a Monotype keyboard. This was a machine something like a giant typewriter, except that, unlike a typewriter, it had a key for every letter of the alphabet in both capitals and lower case and in italics, bold and small capitals. It was powered by compressed air and punched holes in a paper tape. These holes were coded A to N and 1 to 15 and each combination was unique to a letter of the alphabet. For example A6 represented one letter and D14 another, and so on.

Each character was allocated a unit value, from 5 to 18 and the measure on the keyboard was set taking into account the number of units in a given pica measure. Therefore 20 ems of 12 point contained 240 units while the same measure in 6 point contained 480 units. As each key was struck a rack moved along, counting off the widths of the various

Monotype keyboard and caster

characters. At the same time, each time a space key was struck a pointer moved up on a cylinder which was relevant to the type size being used. At 4 ems from the end of the line the cylinder started to rotate tape and when there was no more room for another word a reading was given which set the width of the spaces for that line.

Paper tape and justifying scale

When completed the paper tape was taken to a Monotype casting machine where it was placed on a cylinder containing a row of 32 holes. Compressed air was blown through these holes and only passed through the perforations in the tape. This caused a matrix case holding 225 characters in fifteen rows of fifteen characters, numbered A to N and 1 to 15 as in the keyboard, to be positioned over a mould through which hot metal was pumped and which produced the relevant character. As the last piece of paper tape to be produced on the keyboard was the first to go through the caster the space setting was fixed before the line was cast, resulting in a perfectly justified line of type. I was given a dummy keyboard and a book full of exercises to take home and practise in my spare time. These exercises were very boring and repetitive in the early stages as they were designed to educate the fingers to seek out certain keys without having to look at

them. The exercises were designed to gradually work through a series of random letter combinations to sentences which contained every letter of the alphabet such as "the quick brown fox jumps over the lazy dog" and "dexterity in the vocation of typesetting may

Mould (left) and matrix case

be acquired by judicious and zealous work". Had I received a pound for every time I typed one of those lines I could have retired early as a very rich man.

Eventually, due to men being called up for military service, there was a vacancy in the keyboard department and I moved on to the real thing. The keyboard room was a small room on the front of the building containing four keyboards facing into the building. Behind were two large windows and the working conditions were very good, with natural daylight falling over one's shoulder on to the copy from which one was setting. The operators were seated on comfortable adjustable office chairs and each man had a small table with a single drawer in which to keep his personal belongings.

There was Bill Flory, the working foreman, Roy Carter, who had been declared unfit for military service, and occasionally one of the readers, who had been a keyboard operator in the past, came in to help out. One of these was Bert Bentley. Bert used to sit there tapping away, a trilby hat perched on the back of his head, whistling "O sole mio" in a most doleful tone. Everyone worked hard in the keyboard room, but occasionally we relaxed with a bit of horseplay. The keyboards used spools of paper and every key which was struck punched two or three holes, so at the end of the day there were thousands of little bits of paper known as chads. These were emptied out of the machine by means of a suction device and usually consigned to the waste paper basket. However, they were in great demand for use as confetti at weddings and a separate box was used for these. Sonny Mansfield's reading box was situated just above the keyboard room and there was a hole in the ceiling to allow a pipe to go through. Occasionally we would extend a spool of paper into a tube, fill it with chads, put one end against the hole in the ceiling, and insert a compressed air pipe into the other. There would be cries of "snowstorm Sonny!" as his room was filled with thousands of tiny chads. Sonny used to thump on the floor and shout out "you daft beggars".

These chads were also used in other ways. One could open one's drawer in the morning and suddenly find oneself covered in them. During the night someone had attached a string to the back of the drawer which led to a box of chads perched on top of one of the light fittings. As soon as the drawer was opened down came the chads. Or maybe when a drawer was opened someone on the other side of the room might be the recipient.

Sometimes the language became a bit strong and then Sonny would come down and complain that the young lady who was his copy holder was upset by it. So we instituted a swear box. Every time Sonny thumped on the floor because of the language the offender had to put some money in for the Spitfire Fund. This raised quite a sum of money in the initial stages but as it became more expensive to swear the bad language abated and the fund suffered as a result.

It was about this time that I had my first girl friend. She was a pretty, black-haired girl who worked in the binding department on the other side of the yard. I used to smile at her occasionally but I was very shy in those days and didn't dare to ask her out. One evening I was at the cinema when I saw her some rows away. When she left I followed her to the car park and saw her get on a bus to one of the outlying villages. I too boarded the bus, which was quite full, and got off when she did. She was talking to one of the other passengers and I lost my nerve and faded away into the darkness. The following week I told her what I had done. "Next time I'll wait for you" she said. This gave me the courage to ask her if she would go to the cinema with me. To my delight she agreed.

Then followed about three months of bliss, taking her to the cinema and to parties, but as I was an impecunious apprentice we always had to walk home afterwards. We had long, moonlit walks and spent many happy moments exchanging hot passionate kisses while leaning against a five-barred gate.

She must have been a very tolerant and understanding young lady. One Saturday I took her to a party which involved walking five miles there and five miles home again afterwards and she didn't complain. She was also very tactful. I had bought a new tie which in retrospect was cheap and flashy, but I was proud of it. I asked her if she liked it. She replied that she liked it because I had bought it. Two weeks later she bought me a much more sober tie for Christmas.

Then one day she told me that she was going to go out with another man, a man a few years older than us, and with obviously more experience in the ways of the world and with money in his pocket to treat her to all sorts of things I could not. I was devastated. The bottom had dropped out of my world, or so I thought. But this was a necessary learning experience and I quickly recovered from this seemingly mortal blow. I had now tasted the delights of courting and looked forward eagerly to the next nubile young girl I could hold in my arms.

One evening we were out courting when the air raid sirens sounded. It was my night on duty so I quickly walked the young lady home and then hurried the four miles back to my village and reported for duty. There was not much going on — the odd plane flying over and some desultory gunfire for a short time and then nothing for a couple of hours. Then the main wave came over and the air was full of the noise of aeroplanes and bursting shells and the sky in the direction of London was glowing red from numerous fires and peppered with thousands of starlike flashes from the anti-aircraft barrage.

Suddenly, distinct from the general noise, came a sound like heavy rain falling and the next minute a wall of flame and smoke appeared at the far end of the village. My fellow warden Les and I grabbed a bucket of water and a stirrup pump and raced to where the fire was and discovered that most of the incendiary bombs, for that is what had made the noise, had fallen on the railway line but one was embedded in the roof of the rectory. We immediately got to work to contain the fire and stop it spreading. In the meantime the rest of the wardens and fire watchers had arrived and one managed to find a garden rake and pulled the incendiary bomb off the roof on to the driveway where it was easily dealt with.

We were aware that the vicar was standing beside us watching the proceedings, resplendent in striped pyjamas, woollen dressing gown, and a loud-checked golf cap. Somebody asked "any more about sir?" "Yes, there's one on the bed" he replied quite casually. We rushed into the house and up the stairs and sure enough there was a bomb on the bed which was blazing away merrily. It must have come down the chimney. One of the senior wardens got down behind the landing wall with the hose while the rest of us took it in turns to pump from the foot of the stairs. He told us afterwards the thoughts that had been going through his mind. "Is that an ordinary incendiary bomb or it is one of the explosive kind?" "Is this a brick wall or is it just a partition?" Fortunately it was just an ordinary incendiary bomb and it was soon under control and the fire put out. Meanwhile, in the grounds, the fire watchers had been piling earth on to other bombs and smothering them while the ones in the field and on the railway track were gradually dying away. This sort of incident was fairly frequent in the Hertford area as many of the bombers were unwilling to fly through the barrage and turned back, dropping their bombs at anything which showed, like a railway line or river.

When this excitement was over I suddenly realised that the head cold from which I had been suffering had completely disappeared!

Meanwhile I was enjoying my time in the keyboard department. Whereas up till now I had been merely handling work of various kinds, correcting, making up pages, etc., I was now able to read the copy as I was setting it up. As the work we handled covered a wide variety of subjects, from technical magazines to poetry and fiction, I was not only learning about my job but also about the use of language and all sorts of facts which would add to my general knowledge. Just to give one example. One of the monthly magazines dealt with mining in its various forms all over the world. I learnt a lot about open-cast mining, drift mines, adits, how dehydration was combated in the deep mines of South Africa by adding small quantities of salt to the drinking water, how the mining companies contributed to the economy of the country by providing decent housing for the workers and helping to control malaria and sleeping sickness by regular spraying of the mosquito-infested swamps of the region.

This particular magazine had a personal column which related to the whereabouts of mining personnel throughout the world, for example, "John Smith has returned from the Gold Coast", or "Joe Brown has taken up an appointment in Sierra Leone", etc., and these items came on scraps of paper of all shapes and sizes. Our foreman, Bill Flory, was a keen walker and went to the Lake District every year for his holiday. On one such occasion which, it must be stated, took place some time later than the other events described in this paragraph, Eric was setting the personal column and on a whim typed in "Bill Flory is on holiday in the Lake District". Some time later one of the readers walked in with a broad grin on his face and said he'd been looking everywhere for the relevant piece of copy.

Chapter Four

The mysteries of the Orient

Work in the case room had been very physical, involving lifting cases of type weighing about eighty pounds and formes which could weigh a hundredweight or more, but keyboard work was entirely sedentary. I was concerned that the fitness I was acquiring through hard work would deteriorate if nothing was done about it, so I embarked on a programme of physical fitness. I joined the Health and Strength League, not to be confused with the League of Health and Beauty, and began a course of judo and self defence with Jim Harpham, one of their instructors. Apart from the self-defence instruction Jim introduced me to weightlifting, both as a sport and as a means of muscular development. Initially, however, I limited myself to a two-mile run before breakfast every morning. This involved leaving the village via a steep hill, running along a road for about three-quarters of a mile, and returning through some woods and parkland. It was a wonderful experience on a Spring morning, with a blue sky and dew on the grass, to run across the field after leaving the road and smell the delightful perfume of the lilac in bloom in the park. Initially this run took about twenty minutes but as I became fitter I used to manage it in fifteen. As soon as I arrived home I stripped off in the kitchen and sponged myself down with cold water, followed by a brisk rub down with a towel. In addition to this, every lunchtime I drank a pint of cold milk, bought from the dairy opposite, and each evening a bottle of milk stout. I sailed through the day feeling on top of the world.

After a spell in the keyboard room I had to go into the Monotype casting department for a few months, one reason being that it was part of my general training but the other more important aspect was that I could see at first hand what happened because of keyboarding errors. The casting room had four composition casters, which were used for casting work produced by the keyboards, and a super caster, the prime purpose of which was to produce large display type and strips of rule and lead to be used in the composing department. Each caster had a gas-fired metal pot and the room was very hot and noisy, especially during the summer months. The prime job of the caster attendant was to make sure that the type was being cast correctly, to inspect it regularly to ensure that the metal was clean and smooth, and to see that the lines were of the correct length. He also had to keep the metal pot topped up by inserting slabs of metal, which was a composite of lead, tin and antimony. This meant holding the slab of metal and lowering it gently into the pot so as not to reduce the temperature drastically and finally letting go as it became too warm to hold. It was extremely important to keep the metal dry as the smallest drop of moisture on the metal slab would produce a violent reaction in the metal pot, resulting in hot metal splashing all over the place.

We were at that time producing a vast amount of propaganda work for the government, much of which was directed towards the Arabic speaking countries. Type wore out quickly, especially the more commonly used characters and there was a limit to the number of times that type could be "dissed". The original type came from Germany which meant that it was impossible to purchase more and the situation was becoming desperate. One of our directors, Mr. Stanley Harrison, was a clever inventor, and he had devised a way of making and casting Arabic type by inserting a character into a piece of wood, with a critical amount showing above the wood surface and placing this in a tank of sulphuric acid in which copper rods were suspended. The acid was agitated by paddles turned by a small electric motor which caused the copper to grow round the piece of lead. The resulting piece of copper was then trimmed on a lathe to produce a matrix. As many of the Arabic characters are joined to their neighbours on one or both sides the character overhung the body of the type and these projections had to be filed off, a time-consuming operation. This was originally carried out by two ladies, known as the filing ladies, who sat and filed these characters day in, day out, before placing them in paper bags. It was not long before Mr. Harrison invented a machine to do the work. All the ladies had to do then was to keep the machine loaded, still a very boring job but considerably faster.

To produce 72 pt. (1 inch) type he had purchased an old upright type caster. This worked by placing a piece of wood on a pin in the mould, which reduced the weight of type and also saved precious metal, bringing the matrix down over the mould and pulling a lever which allowed the pump to send a measured amount of metal into the mould. Mr. Harrison approached the machine from behind a wicker shield with a small window in it, pulled the lever and beat a hasty retreat. Then followed a few grinding noises, an almighty bang when pieces of hot metal flew all over the room, and one piece of type was cast.

Les Wright was the foreman of the casting room and his brother Arthur also worked there. They both knew their job thoroughly but whereas Les was strictly professional and was concerned with the smooth running of the section, Arthur was a practical joker. One of his favourite tricks was to hold a pair of tweezers in a metal pot for a few seconds to make them hot and lightly touch someone on the elbow with them. This was guaranteed to make one jump a mile. Then, half an hour or so later, he would again touch the same spot with something cold, with exactly the same result. Each morning before beginning casting the metal pots had to be cleaned of all dross and this was done by stirring in a piece of tallow which brought all the dross to the surface where it could be skimmed off. Arthur, on occasions, placed a small piece of tallow on top of the pot and let it smoke while he tucked a cloth into his shirt collar and pretended to be frying chips. With the room full of tallow smoke everybody left cursing except for Arthur, who thought it all a huge joke. Fortunately I only spent a few months there and went back on the keyboards.

Partly because the company had to make a regular report of my progress to the Wallinger Trustees, which meant they had to be seen to be giving me a proper apprenticeship, I was soon moved on, this time to the Oriental Department, under the watchful eye of Bert Smith. Bert had spent years composing oriental type and was familiar with such exotic languages as Arabic, Persian, Amharic, Chinese, Japanese, Greek, Hebrew, Tamil, Burmese, Cyrillic, and a host of other non-Latin languages. This didn't mean that he could speak any of them but he fully understood what each character was and in which context it should be used. Also on the ship were Jimmy Childs, a gentle man for whom nothing was too much trouble to explain, Charlie Groves and Frank Eames, two senior apprentices who were awaiting call-up for the army, and three other boys of about my age, Alex Reynolds, Les Hawkins, and Ivan Hawksworth. With that number of apprentices on one ship life must have been very difficult for Bert at times. We loved to whistle while we worked and Les, in particular, whistled jazz. Sometimes we whistled in unison and at other times whistled our own tunes so one can imagine the cacophony of noise. We'd see Jack Boughton frowning from the magazine ship and then he'd go over and have a word with Bert who'd tell us to "give it the breeze".

My first task was to learn the layout of the Arabic type cases and the names of the various characters. I soon became familiar with ains, waws, hamzas, and tashdids. Many of the Arabic letters had four different forms, known as initial, medial, final connected and final unconnected. There were two sizes — 13 point, which was just over one-sixth of an inch and 17 pt. which was about a quarter of an inch and as the characters were very narrow it took a long time to compose a page. A column of Arabic, about twenty inches long, took about six hours to compose, and this amounted to just over a printed page, or perhaps two if illustrations were used, so it was very labour intensive. An important tool was a small flat file to smooth off any small projections which had been missed by the filing machine.

There were two kinds of Arabic, pointed and unpointed. Pointed Arabic, which had all the various accents and symbols round the basic letters, was the most difficult to set up as the accents had to be set in a different line in 3 point type. This was the kind of Arabic used for children's books. The unpointed variety was the most commonly used and the pronunciation was taken for granted by the reader. In some cases accents were soldered on to characters by Harry Hall, a skilled engraver who managed the foundry. This was a job which gave little room for error as he was soldering lead to lead and the smallest amount of excess heat would melt the character.

The setting of Chinese was mostly undertaken by Jimmy Childs. There were twenty-four cases of type, divided into dozens of small compartments containing characters and identified by a number. Two minutes was allowed for the finding and placing of each character which was achieved in the following manner. A large book, containing a drawing of every character, and which had been made by the previous works manager, Mr. Kenneral, was first consulted. Every Chinese character contains a basic part, known as a radical, and these were drawn at the front of the book. Having found the radical the book then directed one to the pages of characters containing this radical. One then had to search through this section until the required character was found, go to the case containing the character with that number, take it out and place it in the composing stick. In practice some of the characters were common and became familiar to a skilled compositor and in many instances he could go straight to the character without consulting the book.

The dance at Ware Drill Hall was a favourite venue for Saturday evenings. My parents were a little dubious about letting me go at first as the Drill Hall had a certain reputation for drunkenness and fighting. However, as I would be going with a group from the village, they agreed. The first time we cycled the four miles to Ware and chained our cycles together at the back of the Drill Hall. The dance had just started with a quickstep and Sidney Rumbelow's Band was playing "The Darktown Strutter's Ball". The double bass was thumping away and I can still recall the excitement of the moment.

I had little idea of dance steps but Edith Hillyard, the sister of my friend Peter, patiently taught me the basic steps. After that it was a matter of practice. There were instances of fighting and drunkenness of course but they did not include or affect us in any way.

One evening a serious incident was narrowly averted. There were usually large numbers of American servicemen at the dance. On this occasion a Scottish highland regiment had returned on leave from North Africa and were stationed nearby. Naturally many of them came to the dance, resplendent in their kilts. There were one or two wolf whistles from the Americans but as it was early in the evening and not much ale had been consumed these were studiously ignored. Later on, however, some remark was made about the "men in skirts" and suddenly the Americans were lined along one wall and the Scots along the other. Girls were screaming as everyone cleared the floor. Things were looking very ugly.

Then, as if by magic, two American military policemen appeared in the doorway. They just stood there, looking around and holding their long white batons in front of them. Gradually the tension eased, people turned around and started talking, one or two started to dance, and very soon things returned to normal.

At the end of the dance we would collect our coats from the cloakroom and venture out into the blackout and try to locate one another. All around there would be couples embracing in corners and contracts being made regarding the expectations for escorting someone home.

There is one other aspect of the dances which I must mention and that is the subject of drinking. When I hear youths going home late at night singing and shouting because they have had too much to drink, I think back to my own youth. We would drink in the dance hall and during the interval go to one or two of the pubs in the town. We would consume large quantities of beer, albeit much weaker than it is today, and be full of bravado. I can only recollect being drunk once and although I do not recommend drinking to excess I think that everyone should experience being drunk just once so as to be able to appreciate how awful one can feel.

When winter arrived we used to go to Ware by train. We walked into Hertford to the East Station. Usually there was no one around so we simply boarded the train without a ticket. At Ware, instead of going through the station we left via the level crossing. At night we again boarded the train without being stopped and at Hertford, where there was always a ticket collector to meet the last train, we would press a threepenny piece into his hand and walk through. He was happy and so were we. The really unscrupulous used to walk along the platform, cross the goods yard, and climb over the railings.

The carriages in those days had compartments and to ensure that we had one to ourselves we always made sure we had a penny in our pocket. When the train arrived we quickly entered a compartment, closed the door, and held the penny in a small slot behind the door catch. This effectively locked the door and anyone trying the handle would think that it was locked and quickly move on.

On occasions, perhaps because of bomb damage further along the line, the train failed to arrive. After waiting in vain we then had the four mile walk home or, in the case of those from Birch Green or Cole Green, five or six miles. I would arrive home so tired that I would sit in a chair and just stare at my feet. After about ten minutes I would take off one shoe and then, after a further five or ten minutes, take off the other and eventually climb the stairs to bed. In spite of this my parents never heard me come in, apart from one occasion when I thought there was one more stair to go and there wasn't!

When I was about seventeen-and-a-half an event occurred which would radically change the course of my life. We all at some time in our lives reach a point where the paths diverge and we have to make a decision whether to go left or right. This time the decision was made for me.

My friends were gradually being called up for the armed forces and were arbitrarily selected for either the army or navy or air force. My friend Tom French and I decided that if were going into the forces then we would go into a branch which we wanted. We were both very fit at the time and were eager to "have a go". I had been spending three evenings a week with three other friends exercising with weights, practising judo throws, wrestling and cross-country running. So one late autumn morning Tom and I set off for the recruiting centre at Deansbrook Road, Edgware, Tom to volunteer for the Royal Air Force and I for the Royal Marines. The act of volunteering was a bit of an anti-climax as all that happened was that our names and addresses were taken, together with our age and preferences. Nevertheless we felt quite elated and travelled into central London for a meal at Lyons Corner House. Both having very healthy appetites we took two of every course from the self-service counter and travelled back to Hertford feeling comfortably full and contentedly pleased with the day's events.

Some weeks later we were called for our medical. It was a cold day with flurries of snow and we sat about in the large hall wearing only our jackets and trousers, feeling the icy blasts of air every time someone opened the doors to the street. Eventually, however, the medical was over and I had to go before the naval officer in charge of recruiting. He told me that there were no vacancies in the Marines at present but that there were in the Royal Navy. I discovered later that two of our large warships had been lost in the Pacific and that the Navy was short of sailors. He asked me if I knew either Morse or semaphore. I said "Yes, I had learnt semaphore in the Scouts" so he asked me if I would sign on as a signaller. Because I was so keen to get into action I did just that.

Shortly afterwards Tom was called up for the Royal Air Force, only to be transferred to the army a few weeks later. I had to wait for what seemed an eternity until one morning a small buff piece of paper arrived by post telling me to report to H.M.S. Royal Arthur at Skegness two weeks later. I was over the moon. Things were at last happening. Later that day I went into the works manager's office and told him that I would be leaving the following Thursday. "You're going nowhere boy" he said and picked up the telephone and dialled a number. He told me that because of the importance of the work we were doing and the shortage of manpower I had to stay put, setting up Arabic and Persian for the government's propaganda machine. I felt devastated and made an appointment to see the Rev. Roland Smith, who was chairman of the trustees of the Wallinger Charity which controlled my apprenticeship. I felt that he would be sympathetic for he had two sons of his own in the Navy. He told me that there was nothing he could do and that if I defied the works manager and went to Skegness anyway I would only be sent back. My mother was of course delighted. In retrospect I should be glad that I was spared the horrors and tribulations of countless thousands of men and women but at the time it was a terrible blow to my morale and self-esteem. A sad footnote to this was that my friend Tom was killed on a training exercise on Salisbury Plain, the only one of my school friends to lose his life.

Eventually, however, I adjusted to the routine and at the age of eighteen I started to alternate daytime working with night work. This was a novelty at first but it was very lonely working on the top floor of an old building with the windows blacked out and only about five other people in the whole of the factory.

It was a long night, from nine o'clock in the evening till eight o'clock the following morning, five nights a week, and very soon this began to take its toll on my eyes. I would find myself falling asleep reading the newspaper and duly went for an eye test. From this point on I would have to wear glasses for all reading work. My grandmother, who was eighty, complained to me one day that her eyesight wasn't what it used to be as she now had to wear spectacles to read the newspaper!

One of the items we produced was a weekly newspaper for Bengali seamen. Copy was sent to us by rail, but always bearing a postage stamp, with the message "Herewith the lot. More tomorrow." Because it was sent by rail the stamps were unfranked and were known as "Spitfires" because all unfranked stamps were given to the "Spitfire Fund" to help pay for more fighter planes. The editor, Mr. Gupta, used to come down near the end of the week to finalise the copy and he quickly became addicted to Bert Smith's snuff.

Jimmy Childs and Ivan Hawksworth were not called up and soon Charlie Leete was released from the air force to enable us to meet the production demands of the government. We worked many hours overtime and with every other night on duty if the air raid alarm sounded it was a very tiring time. However, we took it all in our stride and continued to make the best of life. One of our treats when we were working overtime was to have tea at Wiltshire's Café. This was usually jam on toast or dripping on toast with a cup of strong tea or, if we were lucky, soft roes on toast, a real luxury in those austere days. On one occasion a detachment of Indian troops joined us for tea. Some of them spoke a little English and were gentle-mannered men from the Himalayas and we spent our half hour painfully trying to converse with them. Occasionally we had tea at Georgette's, a more superior café almost next-door to the factory. Jimmy Childs was a friend of Georgette and she kept open especially for us. It was a little more expensive but it avoided a long wait while others were being served.

Eventually the war ended and men started returning from the forces. There were lots of strange faces to get used to and some mixed feelings at first when they discovered that I had not been in the forces but when they realised that I had had no choice in the matter everything was fine. A new era had begun.

Chapter Five

The post-war period

For a while things went along quietly as men were reabsorbed into their pre-war jobs but some changes were inevitable. Another keyboard had been acquired for the Monotype department to cater for the men who had been demobbed. Soon afterwards though, Roy Carter decided it was time he moved on and left for a job at another company. I was returned to the Monotype keyboard department to join Les Waller and Eric Mead, recently demobbed from the army, and Don Brace, who had been in the air force, together with Bill Flory, the foreman. This was a great team and work once again took on a happy, carefree type of existence. Although there was no sort of incentive scheme we all worked hard, it being a matter of pride to see how much one could do in a given time.

It was round about this time that my brother decided that he too would like to become a printer. After his usual introductory period he came to work on the oriental ship and became proficient in a number of the languages. Eventually he became a reader and apart from a spell when he emigrated to New Zealand for a few years he worked at Stephen Austin's until he retired.

One particular time, we had all been working flat out for about a month and things had to break. One of the men tied a wiper into a knot and hurled it at one of the others. There was immediate retaliation and soon the room was filled with flying wipers. Suddenly it was noticed that Don was still working. "I'll soon put a stop to that" said Les and hit Don on the back of the neck with a well-aimed shot. With that Don grabbed his keyboard cover and charged across the room towards Les just as Mr. Harrison came through the door with some visitors!

The amount of Arabic work coming into the factory was increasing rapidly so the company decided to send me to the Monotype School in London to learn Arabic setting on the keyboard. The Monotype School was situated near where Gamages store used to be, near Leather Lane. The whole of the surrounding area had been flattened during the blitz and all that remained were streets and low walls where buildings had stood. The course lasted for a week and was quite an experience. For lunch we all went to a small café where the speciality was suet pudding with treacle or jam, known as "plain with treacle or plain with jam". The waiter called the order through a hatch where steam belched through. The other side looked like Dante's vision of the inferno. It was interesting to look around Gamages during the lunch hour and then walk through Leather Lane market and compare prices. Most things were very much cheaper in the market.

On my return to work after the course I had to put my training into practice. This was slow work as, because of the nature of the Arabic alphabet, touch-typing was impossible and characters had to be picked out one at a time. However, this was a vast improvement on setting by hand and in due course I was able to turn out about ten galleys of Arabic in a day, whereas with hand-setting this would have been about one a day.

Arabic only occupied part of my time and we were always busy with a variety of magazines, dictionaries and periodicals. One of our regular jobs was the setting-up of the agendas for the various County Council bodies and I particularly remember one of them stating that gravel extraction in the St. Albans area would be completed in about twenty years' time and after that the land would be returned to normal. Twenty years to me at that time was far into the unforeseeable future. Nevertheless, all that has been achieved and long forgotten.

Somewhere about this time Mr. Skerman, the works manager left, and his deputy, Ted Pamphilon, took command. He decided to inaugurate shift work which involved everyone in the department except Bill Flory. We worked one week on normal days, one week early shift, one week late shift, and one week night shift. The shifts were very long, the night shift being from 9 o'clock in the evening till 8 o'clock the following morning, with two half-hour breaks during the night, but only from Monday till Thursday. This system played havoc with our digestive systems so we asked to be allowed to work a month on each shift instead of a week, and this certainly helped as our bodies had more time to get accustomed to the unusual times of eating and sleeping.

When I was working on the night shift in the summer months I used to go out for a walk as soon as I got home. There was an old gravel pit which was overgrown with shrubs and wild flowers and I liked to lie down among the wild strawberries and doze in the warm morning sun for about an hour before returning home and going to bed.

Initially there was no canteen in the factory so the night shift workers gathered in the keyboard room for their breaks as this was one of the few rooms where there was no metal dust to contaminate the food. One man's regular trick was to ask us if we would like "high tea". He then placed a teacup on the floor, stood on the copy safe, held the teapot above his head and poured. More tea went on the floor than in the cup!

One night one of the men brought in a meat and potato pie for his supper. He was sitting in the corner happily tucking into this and another man sitting on the foreman's chair kept making remarks in an attempt to put him off eating. This had no effect until he lit a cigarette and flicked the spent match across the room. It landed in the middle of the pie. "You've been wanting this all evening" said the first man and with that threw the pie at the offender. The remains of the pie hit the back of the foreman's keyboard, showering potato everywhere. There was a shocked silence for a few minutes and then we all set to to clean up the mess. In the morning when the foreman started work his keyboard slowly ground to a halt as the dried potato clogged up the punch mechanism. He had to strip down the machine and clean every part and was not very pleased. However, he did not report it to management but made some very stong comments about the future use of the room as a dining room.

Eventually the company had a smart new canteen built which was fully staffed during the day. Hot meals and snacks were provided and a ten-minute tea break allowed both in the morning and afternoon. So as not to interrupt production there were three "shifts", a few people going from each department at a time. This system worked much better than the ad hoc breaks and probably production improved as a consequence.

There were about six of us, from various departments, working on the night shift and we met in the canteen at midnight and 4 o'clock in the morning. These breaks were eagerly looked forward to as anecdotes were exchanged and many amusing incidents took place. One such incident involved Ron, from the Linotype department, asking how you could siphon petrol from a petrol tank. Phil, one of the machine minders, spent most of the break explaining in detail how this was done but Ron could not understand. The following break Phil arrived with two milk bottles and a piece of rubber tubing. He filled one bottle with water and placed it on a biscuit tin. He then placed the empty bottle on the table beside it and inserted one end of the rubber tube into the water and sucked at the other end until the water flowed through. He then placed that end into the empty bottle and the water flowed from one bottle to the other. "Now do you understand?" said Phil. "Ah!" said Ron. "But that's water. I'm talking about petrol."

Another time we were just getting seated round one of the canteen tables, which were round metal affairs. I had placed a cup of boiling coffee on the table and sat down on the springy canteen chair. I leaned back slightly and without warning the chair tipped backwards. My feet shot out quickly to regain my balance, striking the underside of the table with a sharp blow, the result of which was to send the cup of coffee into the air in a perfect arc to land upside down in Tim's lap on the other side of the table. The air was quite blue for a few minutes but Tim quickly regained his equilibrium.

We used to get fairly regular visits from the police at night. Word had obviously got round at the police station that we had tea breaks twice during the night and often a young copper would call in "just to see if everything's alright". Then of course they would stop for a cup of tea and a chat. However, it was not a bad thing to have a good relationship with the local police and to know a number of them by name.

One of the things we liked to do in the Spring and Summer was to go for a walk during our second break and this was particularly nice in the Spring when the chestnuts were in blossom and the air was cool and scented. We went back to work feeling invigorated but it was still a long drag till the end of the shift.

Around this time occurred one of the great tragedies of my life. My mother became ill and was diagnosed as suffering from cancer. It was terrible to see her growing gradually weaker. She was so brave. The family were putting on brave faces and trying to give her hope for the future, not telling her what was wrong, but she knew and kept up the pretence for our sakes. I spent as much of my spare time as possible taking her for long walks in a wheelchair until she became bedridden and had more and more frequent visits to the hospital. The night my father came home from the hospital and said that she had gone I just couldn't grasp it for some time. Life is so unfair. After years of struggle bringing up a family, and just as things were getting easier and she could enjoy life, she was struck down. I know this happens to so many people and they can probably understand the bitter irony of it.

The following year I got married and moved to a flat in a converted mansion at Watton-at-Stone. This was a wonderful place to start married life as the house stood in several acres of park land and had a magnificent cedar tree on the lawn. It did, however, involve a five-and-a-half mile cycle ride at the beginning and end of each day which kept me fit but was very tiring at the end of a late shift or night shift. It also meant that I saw very little of my wife except for weekends, as she was leaving for work just as I arrived home in the mornings and I had to leave for work at about eight o'clock in the evenings.

In 1954 Stephen Austin's opened a new factory at Caxton Hill, Hertford. This had been under construction for some time and as areas became ready so different departments moved in. Most of the comps were involved in helping with the laying out of the new factory, siting furniture and equipment and getting a free allocation of beer into the bargain. The keyboard operators and readers had to keep working at the old plant until the last minute when all their books and equipment was rehoused in one day and they carried on with their work with hardly a pause.

The keyboard department was moved by the Monotype engineers whose chargehand, Ernie, was a man of incredible strength. He moved things single-handed which would have required the combined strength of two or three ordinary men. He asked me to help him to lift the copy safe on to the back of the lorry. We each took a handle and he said "on the count of three". We swung the safe into the air and at its apex, when it was weightless, I changed hands to swing it into the lorry. Ernie was horrified at such an act and swore at me for about two minutes non-stop without repeating himself. Translated into plain English what he actually said was "don't ever do that again!"

Eventually everyone was rehoused and it was time for the official opening of the factory on the 10th November 1954. The opening ceremony was performed by John Bonfield, Assistant Secretary of the Typographical Association. This was the first time that such a ceremony had been performed by a representative of the Tyographical Association, another stepping stone in the annals of the association's history. All the employees were assembled, together with invited guests. The Father of the Chapel, Reg Marshall, and two apprentices, "Printers' Devils", carrying a cask of beer between them, were dressed in the costume of 1768, the year the company was formed. After shaking hands with Reg, John Bonfield said "I instruct you, Mr. Marshall, as father of the chapel of Stephen Austin and Sons Ltd., to demonstrate to the assembled company what would have been done by printers in the year 1768 had they been pre-sented with new premises." The father of the chapel and the two apprentices then proceeded to the four corners of the factory and duly "wetted" them with beer in accordance with a quaint old printers' custom. Reg returned to Mr. Bonfield and said: "Mr. Bonfield, I report that the factory has been 'wetted' in the manner of printers of the year 1768." From a silver tankard he then drank the Company's health. The guests were then taken to a celebration luncheon at the Corn Exchange. In the evening the employees, from the cleaning ladies through to senior management, attended a superb dinner at the Shire Hall.

The factory was open plan and it seemed strange at first as we had all been used to our cosy, if somewhat draughty rooms at the old factory. I did not like our new quarters. The room had no windows, only north lights high up in the roof, and it was very noisy. Added to that, because it was no longer considered to be a fire risk, employees were allowed to smoke and cigarette smoke from the two smokers in the department drifted round the room from time to time. It was like working in a goldfish bowl. I decided it was time to move on.

My first move was to the Alcuin Press at Welwyn Garden City as a compositor. It was not my intention to stay there for long but Alcuin was a good melting pot where people from all over the south of England went to work and exchanged information and it was a good place to get to know what sort of jobs were going and where. Watford was considered to be one of the best places to work as the wages were considerably higher there than anywhere else in the area so that was one of the possibilities I had in mind.

I left Stephen Austin's with more than a few regrets as I had enjoyed working there. There was a ceremony when I was presented with a garden syringe, a pair of Rollcut secateurs, and a Thermos flask from my fellow workers.

The following Monday I started my new job. This was mainly magazine work, setting up advertisements by hand and making up pages from monotype. I had been there for only a few weeks when I heard that Creasey's of Hertford were going to install a Monotype keyboard and caster and would be requiring an operator. This sounded a good proposition because of the possibility of future expansion and the prospect of running a small department. I applied for the job and because of my previous association with Stephen Austin the job was mine.

Creasey's was a small jobbing printer in the centre of Hertford and was in the process of expanding. A new factory extension was being built and the whole atmosphere was that of a family firm with Mr. Creasey himself being a rather avuncular figure who was very approachable. As in most printing firms there were several characters, among them Alf Heffer and Pete Jones who talked in broad Irish accents for the first week I was there just to see my reaction. Then there was old Vic, a man who was nearing retirement, but who could handset type at the speed of light. A retired compositor who was stone deaf used to come to see him and they would converse by running their fingers over a case of type, pointing out the letters and using the space box to finish a word. This was done at an incredible speed and although I was a fairly fast typesetter I could not follow them.

All of the work done at Creasey's was hand set which meant a proportion of one's time was spent "dissing" to refill the typecases. There were certain characters, such as full points and commas, which were in short supply and sometimes, after spending the last couple of hours in a day dissing one would come to work the following morning and find that the night worker had emptied all the boxes of full points. Then began a cat-and-mouse game of hiding some of these characters away in a safe place so that one had a plentiful supply the following day, not a very satisfactory way of running a print shop.

Although only a relatively small company they had their own football team which one year reached the final of the league they were in. Because I had had training in first aid and massage I was asked to be their trainer and used to travel with the team every Saturday to villages all around the county. I am not, and never have been, interested in football but it was good to watch my own colleagues' success and feel part of the team. Fortunately there were few serious injuries and most could be dealt with by the magic cold sponge.

I well remember the only Christmas I spent at Creasey's. Mr. Creasey had said that we would finish work at 3 o'clock on Christmas Eve and adjourn to the White Hart for drinks and snacks. Most of us had been out for a pint in the lunch hour and when we got back to work someone had opened a bottle of port which was being passed around and people were beginning the get merry. Just after 2 o'clock Mr. Creasey walked in, took one look, and said: "I'm not going to get any more work out of you buggers today. You'd better tidy up and go over now." Suddenly someone said "Where's the bottle of port?" Someone else said "Where's Tickner?", Tickner being the apprentice. We found Tickner in the washroom, empty bottle in one hand, leaning against the wall and giggling. We wrapped his coat round him and two of the lads guided him to the White Hart where a magnificent spread had been laid out and drinks were on the firm for as long as we wanted to stay there. It was a memorable way to start the Christmas holiday.

After some months at Creasey's I realised that the Monotype installation was not going to materialise. Although very free with his money where social matters were concerned there was not an excess of free cash for reinvestment. A new offset litho machine was purchased and I could see that with this purchase, and the continued improvements to the factory, there would not be enough cash available for the Monotype machines as well. Time to start looking through the advertisements again and this time I was aiming a little higher, at an in-charge job.

I applied for a job as foreman of the Monotype department at the Hereford Times. Mr. Parrott, the assistant works manager, came to Hertford and interviewed me in a local café. We got on very well and he invited me to go to Hereford for the weekend to view the factory, meet the works manager and various other people, and to look at the housing situation. We arranged a time and the following Friday I went to London where I was picked up by the company's van driver, who had been delivering in London, and driven down to Hereford. He took me first of all to see the works manager, Mr. Peacock, at his house. After a short talk during which we arranged for me to tour the factory the following morning he asked me what I was going to do that evening. I said that apart from going out for an evening meal I had no other plans. "Well then," he said, "why not come down to our social club after you've eaten and meet a lot of the people you'll be working with? Our van driver will pick you up. We've got a skittles match tonight."

This I agreed to and in due course I was picked up and driven through the dark streets to the social club. Everyone was very friendly and during the evening I consumed several pints of draught Bass. When the time came for me to return to my lodgings I stepped out of the club and realised that I didn't have a clue as to where the guest house was. Fortunately there was a policeman handy. I remembered that it was near the George Hotel and I knew my way from there and he set me off on the right course.

The following morning I went to the factory and was given the grand tour, after which we got down to discussing the terms of employment etc. It was a nice installation with the sort of work I'd been used to and I would have liked to have worked there but after a tour of the town and the various estate agents I learned that the waiting time for new houses was a minimum of nine months and all the existing houses which came on the market were snatched up by the local cider company. This meant that in addition to my mortgage at Hertford I would have to pay for lodgings for at least nine months. Added to this, if I caught the first train after finishing work on Friday I would be home about 11 o'clock in the evening and would have to leave at 3 o'clock on Sunday afternoon in order to catch the last train back. Reluctantly I had to say "no".

The next advertisement I answered was for a head reader's job, with a new house, at Balding and Mansell at Wisbech, in Cambridgeshire. This appealed to me as the map showed a town right in the middle of countryside, with the sea only a dozen or so miles away. An appointment was made for the date of my twenty-ninth birthday. After a long train journey through mostly flat and uninspiring country I arrived at Wisbech. As I walked through the town to the factory my heart sank. The tide was out and the river was a muddy streak with a trickle of water running through a depressing townscape and by the time I reached the factory I think mentally I had already decided that I couldn't live there. The factory, however, was one of the best I have ever been in, light, airy, and laid out on a production line basis, so that work flowed in a more or less unbroken line from origination to the machine room. There were lots of girls and women working there and as a group they were some of the loveliest I have ever seen. Point in favour.

While I was in the manager's office being interviewed a head appeared round the door and a voice said "See me before you go." It was Dennis Hughes, a man with whom I'd worked at Hertford. He invited me to have tea with him and his wife Brenda after the interview when we could talk freely. He told me he had been trying to get away for about eighteen months and was moving to Dunstable the following week to take up employment at Waterlow's. They had had forty new houses built and were recruiting for all branches of the industry. He gave me a name and address to write to.

Among other things I learned was that no new houses had gone to new employees coming to Balding and Mansell, he himself living in a house next to the factory from where the sound of the machines could be heard day and night. Furthermore there was little or no country to go into as the land was so fertile that most of it was taken up for growing fruit and vegetables and it was a long and tortuous journey to the nearest seaside.

In due course I made my way to the station only to find that the secretary at the factory had got the trains muddled up and the fast train had left an hour before and the one I was going to catch stopped at every station along the way. Eventually I reached Cambridge where I had to change trains. It was a cold breezy night and I had a pint of poor quality bitter at the station buffet to celebrate my birthday. At last the train came in and we set off for the last leg of the journey. It was to be one of those days. At Broxbourne, less than half an hour away from my home station, we were told to disembark as there had been a derailment and passengers to Hertford would be taken by bus. The bus duly arrived and then decided to wait until the next train came in so as to save a journey. I eventually arrived home after 11 o'clock, tired, dispirited, but with a new lead to follow.

I wrote to Waterlow and Sons Ltd. with my c.v. and was told that a vacancy existed for a compositor/reader or compositor/operator which meant that the main work would be that of a compositor but filling in with the other job during holidays and sickness, with the opportunity of it becoming permanent in the event of a vacancy. I decided to go for comp/operator and made an appointment to go to Dunstable. The factory was vast, being about a quarter of a mile long, and built of solid red brick. There were already two comp rooms and a third was being formed specifically to deal with the new magazine and catalogue contracts. A bonus system was in operation which meant that if one worked methodically the basic wage could be increased by as much as thirty per cent.

I had taken my wife with me and at the end of the interview the manager, Albert Aplin, asked if we would like to see the houses. We naturally said "yes" and he took us to see them. These were very large semi-detached houses in Norcott Close, to become known in some quarters as Pica Avenue, because every house was occupied by a printer. They had shared driveways, but we were shown the first one in the road, which had its own drive. Albert said that although the houses were allocated in strict order as people were accepted, as there had been a cancellation, rather than move everyone up, we could have that one if I decided to accept the job. The rent was extremely low, being subsidised by the company, and after a short discussion I accepted. This was to mark the beginning of a new era of my life.

Long service employees of Stephen Austin & Sons Ltd.
Left to right: Miss B. Dowton, G. H. Gostling, W. G. Butler, B. Bentley, F. W. Kimnell, E. H. Pamphilon, H. G. Smith.

Photo courtesy of Herts and Essex Newspapers

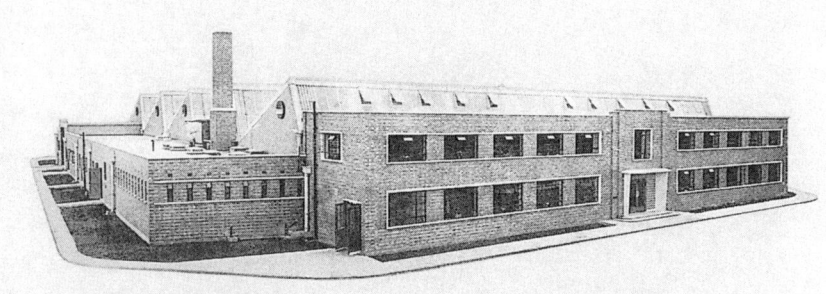

Stephen Austin's new factory at Caxton Hill

Reg toasts the factory

Wetting the factory

John Bonfield cuts the ribbon in the opening ceremony

Chapter Six

The move to Dunstable

The move to Dunstable took place on a cold wet Friday in 1955. My wife was very co-operative and my elder son Keith, who was about two years old, took a keen interest in everything. My younger son Graham, just a few months old, was taken in a carrycot and was blissfully unaware of what was going on. The house seemed like a palace to us. Our first house had been a small two up two down cottage in a terrace opposite a pub and the second one, although slightly upmarket, was still in a terrace, whereas this house was one of the largest three-bedroom semi-detached houses in Dunstable. Furthermore we had a brick-built garage and a reasonable front garden. Even before starting work we felt we had stepped up in the world.

One or two people had already moved in and by the time I went to work on the Monday morning I already felt part of the scenery. The first day was the usual type of induction day, getting to know where things were, being introduced to the bonus scheme and shown how to fill in the various dockets, etc. We had a spacious composing room to work in but, like the other two, it was still run on the old lines of the foreman and his clerk sitting at a raised desk so that he could keep an eye on everyone. Albert was a reasonable foreman, one to whom you could talk and discuss things and I soon felt at home. I quickly became accustomed to the bonus scheme and, although not one of the top earners, my wage packet was considerably heavier than it had been before I moved to Dunstable.

Two things amused me when I first started work at Waterlow's. One was that several of the older men kept their caps and jackets on while working, wearing their aprons over their jackets. The other thing was the local accent. I had heard Bernard Miles many times on the radio talking about Ivinghoe Aston in that broad country accent which was supposed to be a Hertfordshire accent. However, although Ivinghoe Aston is just

The entrance to Waterlow's factory

Photo courtesy of Dunstable Gazette

about in Hertfordshire, the accent is broad Bedfordshire and many of the older men sounded just like Bernard Miles.

As the weeks passed by more and more new people came and we quickly sorted out whom we did and did not want to be particularly close to. Several people came from London and some quickly moved back, saying they did not like the quiet and inactivity of the country. The work was quite strenuous as everything was still composed in hot metal and we probably lifted several tons a day. I was grateful for my earlier weight training as some of the men found this work quite a strain. We handled several topical magazines including a weekly paper for an advertising company, for which they installed a fax machine. This was a very temperamental piece of equipment, nowhere near as reliable as the fax machines we take for granted today. I remember an amusing incident connected with this paper. An advertiser had come up with a new toilet paper and wanted to call it "Rearguard". He apparently hadn't realised the connotations.

Some of us found things a little difficult at times as a number of us had worked at modern printing establishments and were used to modern ways. The attitude at Waterlow's among some of the older men was "We've always done it that way." For example they used to talk about "this accented letter" when they probably meant an é and when setting German they consistently put in the Greek β instead of the German ß.

Most of the new men were placed in the new composing department and the majority of them were good men to work with. Two in particular, John Walter and Wilf Ledger, became my particular friends. John was a gentle giant who had previously played rugby for Bath and still played for the local team, while Wilf was a wiry Yorkshireman with a wry sense of humour. John played rugby union while Wilf was a follower of rugby league and there was many a friendly argument on the merits or demerits of both games. When the rugby league cup final was due to be played at Wembley Wilf obtained four tickets. On the day of the match we set off to Luton station on John's motorcycle combination with me on the pillion, Jim Colquitt, the fourth member of the group in the adult seat of the sidecar and Wilf in the child's seat. When we got to Luton station we had to lift Wilf out of the seat and help him to straighten his legs. We had a good day looking round the West End in the morning, followed by the match in the afternoon. We then returned to the West End for a wash and brush up and a meal and then went to a show. After the show we toured Soho looking at the sights—this was before the Wolfenden Report—and caught the milk train back to Luton. It was interesting to see a lot of the characters depicted in Giles' cartoons and it was obvious that his drawings were taken from real life studies. This day out was so successful that it became an annual event, joined by two of John's friends from the Bath rugby team, Patchy and Clem, and Paul Frost, another rugby union player who worked with us. I was five feet eleven inches tall and weighed thirteen stone but apart from Wilf I was the smallest of the bunch. We were never accosted when we were walking through Soho except for Wilf, who stopped to tie his shoelace and was made an offer he was easily able to refuse. One little pimp approached us and asked us if we were looking for girls. Patchy, who was a huge raw-boned man, leaned over and whispered something in the man's ear. I don't know what Patchy said to him but the man scuttled off as though the hounds of hell were after him.

About this time I joined the judo club at the Empire Rubber Company in Dunstable. We met two evenings a week and Sunday mornings and this exercise, combined with the heavy lifting involved in the comp room, made me very fit indeed. At this period of my life, in my middle thirties, I was probably fitter and stronger than at any time in my life, before or since.

There was a suggestions box in the factory for ways to improve methods of working, safety, etc. and several of us won awards of varying amounts of cash. We had a piece of equipment called a registration table which was a kind of steel table with a moveable screen overhead in which one could adjust the colour parts of a form to register with the master copy. As mentioned in an earlier chapter the type was held in place by means of wooden wedges which were tapped together with a mallet. The moveable screen had an electric cable attached to it and I noticed that this cable was trailing perilously near the metal table and one false blow with the mallet could break the cable and electrocute the operator. I put in a suggestion for a tension arm on the cable and received a small cash award.

One day I was asked to work overtime in the keyboard department on a Saturday morning, which I did. The following Monday I was told that someone had complained to the Father of the Chapel about my working in there and taking some of their bonus. I walked down to the keyboard room and said "I understand somebody complained about my working in here last Saturday." One man, Joe Munts, said "Yes, I did." "Well, in future keep your bloody nose out of my business. I work for

Waterlow's, not for you." We exchanged a few heated words and I walked out. Shortly afterwards one of the other operators said "Watch him. He can be a nasty piece of work sometimes." It turned out that he was the fastest man in the department and earned the highest bonus. However, later on, when I was a full-time member of the department and he found that I was as good and as fast as he was, I earned his respect and we became good friends.

Eventually Bert Green, the foreman of the keyboard department, retired and his deputy Bill Hoare took over. I was then able to go on to the keyboards permanently. There were ten of us in the room, Bill Hoare the foreman, Joe Munts, Ernie Palmer, Dick Charter, Derek Crossley, Jack Wragg, Jeff Loney, Cyril Nind, Johnny Maynard, and me. I quickly got back into my stride as a keyboard operator and was soon earning maximum bonus every week. One of the jobs was the New Testament in various African languages for which a high allowance was given. This was where my training at Stephen Austin's came in as setting foreign languages was second nature to me.

One day I was working away when I became aware of a loud banging noise. Everybody got up and left the room, grabbing anything which would make a noise, and lined up in the gangway. It transpired that an apprentice was coming out of his time. Now at Stephen Austin's when a lad finished his apprenticeship he was expected to take the other apprentices to a small shop near the town hall and buy them all hot drinks and cookies. At Waterlow's, however, things were rather different. They had what was known as a "banging-out ceremony". The junior apprentices were given the morning off work to decorate a forme trolley, usually to a theme which represented the apprentice concerned. At 12 o'clock he was put in the forme trolley by the other lads and wheeled through the various comp rooms, gathering speed as they went. All the journeymen lined the gangway banging on chases, galleys and anything which made a noise. The apprentice was rushed at high speed out of the factory and out of the gates. He then returned as a journeyman.

In the keyboard department there was plenty of overtime at first but gradually the work dried up and we had long periods of sitting about waiting for work. Most of us read to pass the time and books of all kinds were passed around the department, westerns, biographies, fiction, adventure, detective stories. You name it, we read it. Sometimes some of us would go for a whole day without a job. A strict record was kept by the foreman of how long we had been working so that everybody had an equal opportunity to earn bonus. Eventually, however, work picked up and once again we were in full flow.

A new job came in which necessitated us working overtime three nights a week until the job was finished. Sometimes this job didn't come in until about six o'clock and we were lucky to finish before midnight. We worked two nights out of three each week but the long hours soon began to catch up with us. We refused to work after eleven o'clock and found that the work arrived about an hour earlier. We had a short meeting and decided that the work was being held up at the London office, so we then said we wouldn't work after ten o'clock and very soon the work was arriving at four o'clock in the afternoon.

I had been at Dunstable for about four years when the new Downside Junior School was built at the foot of Blows Downs. This was primarily to accommodate the children from the large new estate which had recently been completed. My elder son Keith was one of those relocated from the old Ashton School in the town centre, where he had found the atmosphere somewhat stultifying. The new school, however, had a vibrant headmaster, Ron Fowler, who had handpicked his staff and laid down a strict code of behaviour where no bullying or vandalism was tolerated and very quickly this became a school which was a model for the rest of the county.

John Walter was a member of the Parent/Teacher Association and one day he persuaded me to go with him to an open meeting. The speaker was Les Matthews, site director of the Manshead Archaeological Society, who gave an extremely interesting talk about local history. I was so fascinated by this that I made some enquiries after the meeting and was told that the Manshead was a highly respected amateur society and that membership was open to anyone with an interest in archaeology. I decided to join there and then.

The society's main "dig" during my period of membership was on the site of Dunstable Priory on land owned by Mr.

Stevens, the local ironmonger, and I spent many a happy hour sitting in a trench trowelling away and conversing with the other members, many of whom became good friends.

It transpired that Ron Fowler was chairman of the Manshead Society and by meeting him on the various digs, away from the school environment, I got to know him very well and we became friends. He subsequently persuaded me to stand for the P.T.A. committee and eventually I became Treaurer for a number of years, during which time we raised money to pay for a swimming pool on the school premises, which meant that children could take swimming as a lesson and be back in the classroom shortly afterwards, instead of taking a whole morning or afternoon off to go to the public baths.

One of the local doctors, Dr. Twivy, suggested that there should be a church on the estate which would be a modern church where only the altar would be consecrated and the rest of the building used as a village hall, complete with toilets and kitchen. Residents were asked to buy "bricks" for the church, St. Augustine's, and in due course it was built, complete with plate glass windows. My daughter, Sarah, who came along a few years later, was christened there.

My friend John Walter decided that it was about time I had some transport and persuaded me to buy a motorcycle combination. He came with me to buy one and was very tough with the dealers, telling them that we were not interested in some of the rubbish they were trying to sell us. Eventually he found a motorcycle, a Norton Big 4, which he thought looked a good buy but the chair was shabby. On another motor cycle was a good chair. "Put that chair on that bike and we'll have it" said John. He was very good and spent hours with me driving round Dunstable and Luton teaching me to drive. Eventually I passed my test and was free to travel without recourse to public transport and their restrictive timetables. I could get to Hertford, for example, in an hour, instead of about two-and-a-half hours by bus.

In retrospect, however, my wife and children were very brave to travel in such a flimsy contraption. Motorcycle combinations had a very low insurance and were a very safe form of transport provided one kept one's distance and drove carefully but the occupants of the sidecar were very vulnerable and comfort was at a minimum, especially in the winter when one had to rely on blankets to keep warm.

After about two years I bought my first car. It was a Series E Morris 8 and had belonged to Jim Colquitt who had moved on to something bigger and better. The only thing wrong with the car was a broken front spring and this I replaced myself, lying on my back on the garage floor and heaving on the spring until the eyelets in the end lined up with the hole in the spring attachment, and my wife popping in the retaining pin. I then decided to repaint the car, using Valspar lacquer. I sanded and cleaned the old paintwork down to the bare metal or primer, carefully treating any rust spots until it was ready for painting. Very early one Saturday morning, when the air was completely still and slightly damp, I pushed the car out of the garage on to the previously wetted concrete apron and began painting. Within about ten minutes there were small insects sticking to the fresh paintwork. This was obviously not going to work.

The next move was to wash the inside of the garage, keeping it damp so that no dust could arise, carefully wash and dry the car, and push it into the garage and shut the door. It was very hot but, stripped to the waist, I completed the job that day and the paint dried without anything sticking to it. The car looked unnaturally bright at first but after a few weeks, when the paint had hardened and a few coats of polish had been applied, it looked no different from the original paintwork.

Cyril, one of the keyboard operators, was a car enthusiast, and he persuaded me, over the course of time, to build my own car. This was to occupy my spare time for the next eighteen months. I bought an old Ford 10 from a scrap yard and John towed it home for me. Then began the task of cutting up the old bodywork and stripping it down to its chassis. As it turned out the chassis was rotten and the only things I could use were the engine and gearbox, the steering column, shock absorbers, springs and the back axle. I purchased a boxed-in chassis from the Falcon bodyworks near Slough, had the engine reconditioned, and a higher ratio crown wheel and pinion put in the back axle. The 17-inch wheels were replaced with 15-inch wheels with radial tyres and assembly began. Initially the work was straightforward and there was plenty of help forthcoming from friends and neighbours who were interested in the project. I had taken the back off the old Ford radiator and sloped it according to the instructions and it was now time to order the body. I decided on a sports saloon body in British racing green with a dove grey interior. It was finished to a very high standard but looked huge as it lay on the lawn where the delivery men had left it. With the help of three friends we lifted it into position on the chassis and for the first time we had some idea of what the finished product would look like.

The Ford Falcon Bermuda

The real work now began. The first job was to secure the body to the chassis which would have been easy had the chassis not been boxed in. There were holes in various parts near where the bolts came through but trying to hold a washer and nut with two fingers and pushing the bolt through with the other hand, while at the same time lying in a contorted position, proved very difficult. Eventually a friend who worked at Vauxhall Motors made me a specially shaped spanner which held the nut in position, leaving both hands free. Now the interesting part began, putting in the instruments and wiring. The car body had a built-in hooded dashboard with a plain flat surface. I decided on Smith's 2-inch instruments and from their catalogue cut out the full-size dials and stuck them in position.

61

When I was satisfied I then had to cut out the holes with a hacksaw and file. I ordered the instruments from Smith's, together with a calibrated sports speedometer and set to work. As the weeks went by it began to look more like a production model.

Eventually the car was ready for the inspector to come and pass it for registration. There were some very good car electricians not far from where I lived and I decided to ask them to check the wiring before the inspector came. After they had finished I asked them if it was alright. "Everything's fine" they said, "but it won't start." I had missed out one small wire about three inches long from the carburettor to a condenser. They had, however, fixed it, and the car was now ready for inspection. It was registered without any problem and now came the time for the first road test. I decided to drive to some friends who lived about ten miles away. The car handled well but, when I arrived at my friends' house and stopped, steam was coming from under the bonnet. I lifted the bonnet and looked at the radiator. It was nearly dry. Their neighbour was a test pilot who had built his own Lotus from a kit and he said I needed a cross-flow radiator on that kind of car.

I purchased a cross-flow radiator and although this improved things I still had problems with overheating if the car was stationary in traffic for any length of time. A local sports car dealer said I needed a header tank and he could make one for me to fit under the bonnet. With the header tank fitted I thought my problems were solved but then found that the force of the water coming from the engine bubbled out of the header tank. It needed something to baffle the flow. A thermostat seemed to be the answer but the Ford thermostat was too long. I solved this problem by cutting off the bottom of the thermostat tube and from that moment the car behaved perfectly, never overheating even under the most extreme conditions.

In 1962 the company announced that it was going to purchase some revolutionary machinery for typesetting and that a number of keyboard operators would be retrained to operate it. The machinery would be three high-speed Linotype Elektrons operated by coded paper tape which was to be produced on teletype machines and which would be justified by computer. There were already two old conventional Inter-type machines, which were virtually the same as Linotype, and it was proposed that the three men who currently operated them would run the new machines. There was a rather heated meeting with the manufacturers who assured everyone that these machines constituted no threat to their jobs. It was a case of moving with the times. A number of us were selected for retraining and duly went to London for a course on tele-typewriters which we found heavy and clumsy after our familiar keyboards. At the same time the company advertised for a supervisor to take charge of the whole installation. I applied for the position, was short-listed, and eventually appointed. This was my first step on the promotion ladder.

Training went ahead, a new room was built to house the installation with one end partitioned off for the keyboard section and computer and the rest for the linotypes, benches, galley racks, etc. In the meantime I had to attend further courses on the computer and the Linotype machines in order that I had a complete knowledge of all that went on as it is often the practice of men to try to pull the wool over the eyes of supervisors.

The keyboards were Fairchild teletype machines which were an improvement on the ones we had trained on, having electric keyboards which were light to the touch, and were known as "gutless wonders" because there was very little machinery inside them. They produced a six-channel paper tape (*right*) known as "idiot tape" which was a complete misnomer as it contained all the neces-sary punctuation but no line endings, type size or line length. They had one 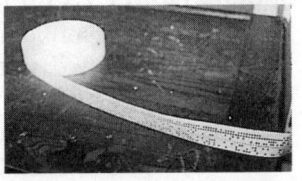 fault, if fault it was, in that they contained a selenium rectifier which occasionally used to burn out, resulting in a most disgusting smell.

Later we purchased an electronic keyboard from Purdy-Mackintosh of Watford. Ron Mackintosh was a great inventor, using the technology of the time, and produced this particular keyboard which used two banks of microswitches to actuate the keys. There were certain things we needed to incorporate to facilitate easier keying, among them being the need to replace the shift/unshift function of the Fairchild keyboards with secretarial shift which was not only a more natural action but infinitely faster, and these presented no problem to him.

The computer was a Linasec II computer and its function was to justify the paper tape into the required line length, type face and type size. Each type face was allocated a width plug, which was a plug-in device in which all the characters of the same width were connected to one outlet point. For example, all the figures were 9 units in width and they were connected to other 9-unit characters such as the letter g. Similarly the full point, comma, the letters i and l, all being 5 units in width, were connected together, and so on. The paper tape was passed at high speed over a light source which read the width of each character in turn, at the same time allowing for the minimum space between words. The line length was continually being assessed and when no more words could be accommodated the computer inserted an end-of-line code. At the same time a new justified paper tape was produced on high-speed Westinghouse punches.

It was a very simple computer by today's standards, each circuit consisting of two or three plug-in cards, of which there were several types. If something went wrong, for instance if one punch failed to operate, it was simply a question of finding which cards contained the circuit for the punch and changing a card of the same type. If this failed to work another card was changed and so on until the problem was overcome. The faulty card was then sent back to the suppliers for repair or replacement. Initially we used to send for a computer engineer but eventually if I had a problem he would talk me through it over the telephone or I'd just go ahead and effect the repair myself.

The three linotypes were a problem from day one. I had seen them in the showroom working perfectly, with a highly competent engineer in attendance. One day I happened to call in the showroom late in the afternoon at the end of a demonstration session and the engineer was climbing all over the machine making fine adjustments. We could not afford that luxury in a work situation. The machines were designed for newspaper production, producing narrow columns of type with no changes of measure or type size. We, on the other hand, needed them for general print work, some of which was most unsuitable and should have been produced by more conventional methods.

The machines were controlled by microswitches which had to act in fractions of a second and if one failed to work at the correct speed the machine would come to a shuddering halt. One example: on the conventional linotypes a wire was attached to a cam which at the end of a line pulled the distribution arm out. This was a time-tested method which worked every time. With the microswitch, however, this was repeatedly causing hold-ups, sometimes dropping matrices which then had to be replaced by hand and causing the operators many frustrations. After many complaints the tried and tested mechanical method was reverted to.

I rapidly discovered that line management was the hardest job in print. Not only was there pressure from above to get work out on time, but there was pressure from below and from the unions. The first instructions I had to give out, especially considering I was giving them to men who had been my colleagues a few weeks before, caused many a twist of the gut, but eventually one becomes case-hardened and I found that by asking, instead of telling, the same results were achieved.

The works manager, Cliff Hardy, and the composing room manager, John Inch, suggested that I should join the Printing Management Association, to further my circle of contacts and enjoy the camaraderie of managers from other printing firms in the area. We met at the Sun Hotel, Hitchin, once a month and had some interesting talks on various aspects of printing.

At that time advances were being made in the fields of cold typesetting, which involved using electric typewriters with interchangeable typefaces and producing camera-ready copy, and phototypesetting, some of which methods were very crude in their early stages. Problems persisted with the Elektrons and eventually management decided to move forward and ordered the IBM MT/SC system which involved using an electric typewriter with interchangeable golfball typeheads.

The Linotype Elektrons reverted to being operated manually and the Fairchild operators returned to the Monotype keyboard department.

Chapter 7

The early days of computer typesetting

I was put in charge of the IBM department with a new staff of younger men with no fixed ideas and Martin Bodsworth was appointed as my deputy. Martin was a bright young man, not long out of his apprenticeship, where he had shown a number of talents, among them a flair for design. The Printing Management Association had set a competition for apprentices in the branch to design a menu for their annual dinner which had to incorporate the PMA logo and colours. Martin designed one in the shape of a wine bottle with the details of the dinner on the label and the logo on the neck label. The bottle opened up to show the menu on the left-hand side and the toast and guest list on the right-hand side. He won the competition, and we were all very proud of him.

I first had to attend a course at IBM at Winchmore Hill where we were taught how to use the equipment by young ladies who were known as educational service reps (ESRs). This was quite a daunting experience for them as they knew little about print and were teaching a group of experienced printers. That week we both learned a lot from each other.

I returned from the course to find that the company had already taken a job for the system which was yet to arrive. I was, however, able to contact a man whom I had met on the course who owned a small IBM set-up in London and he said he could do the job for us. It was arranged that I take the job up to him and take Martin with me for the experience. I had a long-standing invitation to visit the London School of Printing from two people who worked there, so I arranged to combine the two visits.

We duly delivered the job to the small factory somewhere at the back of Liverpool Street station and were told to come back for it after 3 o'clock. As we were handing over the copy a tin can fell from a shelf high up on the side of the factory wall. We looked up and my colleague said "Oh, that's just a rat." Apparently it was commonplace in London. We were thankful that we worked in the country.

We then made our way to the Elephant and Castle for our visit. After enjoying a comprehensive tour of the Printing College we were entertained to lunch by our hosts. Afterwards they said they had to get back to their duties and as there was still about an hour and a half before we could collect our work we decided to have a drink at a local pub. This was at the time of flower power and the pub was full of students wearing colourful clothes and flowers in their hair. Martin and I were wearing suits and we kept getting odd glances until about two o'clock when all the students returned to their respective colleges. When we were the only two left, the barman came over to us. "Excuse me, but are you coppers?" he asked. "No," we replied. "Well, they thought you were" he said. I suppose that was understandable. I was fairly well built and Martin was the son of a police sergeant and built like a brick shed and we must have stood out like sore thumbs.

Eventually the equipment arrived and we were able to go into production. This was an immediate success and in addition to producing camera-ready copy we could also produce paper plates for use directly on to a small printing machine for short runs. Copy was typed out in the usual manner on to a magnetic tape and then transferred to another automatic machine which corrected and justified the type-matter into pages. This was then transferred at high speed on to the repro paper or paper plates. We were very fortunate in having Roger Cutler, the IBM engineering supervisor, living in Dunstable and because we required a very high standard of reproduction I could call on him to make small adjustments before he went to work, which saved several hours of waiting.

At some time during this period I took my family on a holiday based in Cheshire. We visited many places of interest in the area including Derbyshire, which was only a few miles away. One day I told the family that we were going to visit Kinder Downfall, which was the largest waterfall in the area. I had mislaid my Ordnance Survey map and had to rely on a road atlas which was fine for locating the area of the waterfall but did not show contours or heights or show distances with any degree of accuracy. We eventually arrived at the end of a lane near the village of Hayfield and set off across the steeply sloping fields. After a short time we realised that perhaps the project was a little too ambitious so I suggested that the family go back to the car and that I would go on and see them in about an hour. I continued up the side of Kinder Low, over Red Brook, and eventually reached the waterfall on Kinder Scout. It was a little disappointing because the weather was dry and not much water was flowing over the edge. However, I looked across the moors, beautiful in a wild and lonely sort of way, and decided to walk on a little way.

I suddenly realised that I was a long way from the car and made my way down off the moors. By this time I was hot and thirsty and feared that I would get it in the neck for being away for so long. In due course I reached the lane which led back to where the car was parked and just a short way along was a lovely stone-built pub, the kind you see pictured on calendars. I went in and ordered a pint and it barely touched the sides. I then had a second which was almost as good and then decided to face the music. When I reached the car there was no one in sight. I eventually found the family enjoying a picnic in a field behind a stone wall. They had decided that in no way would I be back within the hour and were quite happy. I discovered later, when I found the Ordnance Survey map, that I had walked about twelve miles. This reawakened my love of walking and I decided there and then that I would have to walk the Pennine Way.

Then began lots of preparation. I read all the books I could find about the Pennine Way, in particular John Hillaby's *Journey Through Britain* and Wainwright's *The Pennine Way*. I joined the Youth Hostels Association and planned my route around approximately twenty mile stages. After some training sessions which culminated in a thirty mile walk with a back-pack laden with books I felt I was ready. I used my annual two-week summer holiday with the promise that my family would have a holiday at Butlins when I returned.

To say that I enjoyed the Pennine Way would be an overstatement as the part which runs through Derbyshire takes in a number of peat bogs and is just a hard, filthy slog. I also made the mistake of walking twenty-eight miles on the second day which took in some of the worst country in Britain, the idea being to get that part beind me. Another thing I discovered was that a thirty mile walk in Buckinghamshire with a backpack laden with books was nothing like fifteen or twenty miles in the Pennines. However, it got better as the days passed, despite some atrocious weather. I sent a picture postcard home every day with my current progress and the family kept a map with little flags so they knew where I had been two days previously. But the real highlight was when I arrived home. My little daughter Sarah, about three years old, was playing in the garden. She looked up and saw me and calling out "Daddy!" came running towards me and flung herself into my arms.

After this I had caught the walking bug and was soon planning my next long-distance walk. The Ridgeway was the next one on the list, followed by the Offa's Dyke path and the Cotswold Way. These were interspersed with some of the shorter walks such as the Oxfordshire Way, etc. I joined a walking club and very soon walking became a major part of my life and has continued to be right up to the present time.

Back on the work front. One day I was told that somebody from IBM was at the gate to see me. This turned out to be Jane Gray, who was the education supervisor at IBM but who was also our ESR. This turned out to be the beginning of a great business relationship with Jane keeping me up to date with the latest developments and I giving her tips on how the equipment was best used in a printing environment. Over the years we became very good friends. We arranged for her girls to come to the factory to see how a printing works operated and I in return gave some talks at IBM on the application of their equipment.

The tours round the factory were very popular with the ESRs and there were two highlights. One was the passport department. We printed passports for many different countries, all looking very much alike except that real gold leaf was used only for the British passport cover, the rest having a cheaper metallic substitute. The girls were shown the various sample pages and invited to say which was the real gold. They invariably got it wrong but went away happily clutching a cheque book cover as a souvenir of their visit.

The other highlight was the envelope factory which was adjacent to the printing works. Peter Walker, the manager, showed them in detail how envelopes were made and when they came to the gumming machines and saw the buckets of gum standing beside them, which appeared to be seething and having a life of their own, they all vowed they would never lick another envelope. The tour always finished with tea and cakes in the staff canteen.

One thing that struck me about the IBM personnel was that they were all, without exception, extremely likeable and talented people. Jane, for example, had driven all round the world in a Mini and all her girls were a cut well above the average. Perhaps this was part of IBM's strategy — to employ only nice people. Whatever the reason it certainly worked.

One of my instructions around this time was to become an expert on all kinds of keyboards. This involved travelling to various manufacturers, usually in or around London, and trying out their products. At that time many manufacturers were trying to climb on the band wagon and many of their products, while not inferior, did not meet the rigorous standards they were designed for.

I was gradually involved more and more into looking at photo-typesetting developments and was given various assignments which frequently took me away from the factory. This not only improved my knowledge of different aspects of the trade but also gave me many new contacts throughout the printing world.

In addition to these assignments my new position meant that I was able to attend the various computer typesetting conferences. This was an exciting innovation in the printing world, although in retrospect it was very crude as the problem was being approached by various organisations and they did not all appear to be moving in the same direction. Optical character recognition was in its infancy and many things we now take for granted, such as text rotation, reverse video, and layering were only pipe dreams.

Of much greater interest was the International Printing Exhibition (IPEX) which was held every few years. Here one could see the latest developments in real terms and each and every company was only too happy to demonstrate their particular piece of equipment. One really needed at least two days at the exhibition, not only because of the plethora of things to see but because of the number of old colleagues one met.

Waterlow's was a large company and the factory was over a quarter of a mile long. Consequently personal contact between the various managers and supervisors was infrequent. The company decided to start a club for all management, from the managing director down to line supervisors and this was called the Foremen's Club. The club met once a month at the Sugar Loaf Hotel in Dunstable and the meeting usually consisted of three parts: a talk, usually about a particular aspect of printing but occasionally a general interest topic, followed by a discussion, followed by a free discussion, which meant that we adjourned to the bar and the drinks were on the company. This worked very well in the main, with people ordering rounds just as if they were buying them and nobody abusing the system, until one evening when an over-ambitious barmaid was in attendance. No sooner had one put one's glass down than it was immediately refilled and the bar bill that evening was double the usual. It was quite an evening.

There were two managers that evening, whose identities will remain unpublished, who were wearing identical raincoats. The only difference was that one of them was a heavily-built six-footer and the other one was a little over five feet in height and small. The small man decided it was time he went home and put on the wrong raincoat. It was a wet night and the car park at the rear of the hotel had a gravel surface. The man in question tripped over the hem of the raincoat and fell to the ground. Each time he tried to get to his feet he crawled on to the hem of the coat and fell down again. He was discovered some time later very wet and very dirty and the raincoat was completely ruined.

On the same evening one of the night supervisors arrived at work drunk and was dismissed. From that time on the barman was given a certain sum of money to work to and after that you had to buy your own drinks. It was unfortunate if it was your turn to order a round just as the money ran out!

It was found after a time that the composing section of the club always seemed to congregate together round the bar and

71

from this sprang the idea of a comps dinner once a year. Jack Giles, the deputy composing room manager, had lots of contacts in the pub world and he arranged some memorable nights out. One such evening involved the landlady of the pub removing her long johns because she said she was too hot in them. When we got on the coach to go home there they were hanging from the luggage rack. After we had all alighted the coach driver discovered them and thought "I'd better not let my wife see these" so he posted them through Jack's letterbox on his way home. The following morning Jack's mother asked him if he had had a good night. "Yes," replied Jack. "I thought so" said his mother. "I found these on the doormat."

More and more of us found we were being entertained to lunch and were asked to choose the wine. Wine was not so much in vogue as it is today and our knowledge was very limited, so it was decided to form a wine club. Every month we met at the sports pavilion and various wine merchants came down with different wines for us to taste. The first meeting was in November and a representative from the wine merchant Peter Dominic came along with three bottles each of forty different wines, ranging from the very dry to the very sweet. After a short talk the rep said that as it was near Christmas we could find out what we liked and place an order. He suggested that we start with the dry wines and work our way through to the sweet, making notes as we went as to which wines we liked best. Then, as he was not taking any wine back with him, we could finish it off. There were forty of us at the meeting and we finished the lot so that we drank an average of three bottles each. The following morning the nurse had many visits from people wanting a cure for a hangover.

During the course of the following months we enjoyed some very interesting wine tasting sessions. Representatives from different wine companies came and talked about their products and we learned a lot not only about wines but the regional geography of their countries of origin. Sometimes we paid a nominal sum for the evening if the wines were being supplied free of charge. At other times we paid for the wine consumed or paid the expenses of the demonstrator. We had a very good chairman, Charles Hasler, who was an experienced toper and when he left I was invited to be chairman. This was a good experience as it taught me to handle meetings in a friendly atmosphere.

The Foremen's Club was going strong and its chairman was moved from Waterlow's to manage another factory in the group. I was asked to take over the chair for the rest of his term, and at the annual general meeting I was re-elected as chairman for the following year, giving me an almost two-year term of office. This was an enjoyable experience but a little nerve-wracking at the annual dinner when I had to make a speech. However, I had a good friend at IBM who was always able to furnish me with a good after-dinner joke which invariably went down well.

Our works manager, Bob Baker, was one of the nicest men I have ever worked for. With that in mind I asked him if he would chair one of our Foremen's Club meetings where any manager could speak his mind or air his grievances, within the confines of the meeting, without fear or favour. This he agreed to and we had a very good meeting with lots of frank and open discussion. The manager of the Cheque Department, Alf Scott, raised his hand to ask a question. "Yes Alf?" said Bob. "Mr. Baker. I've had two secretaries in the last six months and they've both left because they were pregnant . . ." began Alf. "Bully for you" interrupted Bob.

It was about this time that John Inch decided to move on, leaving the job of composing room manager open. Cliff suggested that I should apply for it. He didn't think that I would get it as Jack, the deputy manager, was a very competent man and was almost certain to get the job, but he said it would show that I was interested in promotion. This turned out exactly as predicted but it gave me the necessary push to start me on the promotion trail. I applied for a job as shift manager at one of the factories in the group which, had I been successful, would have resulted in a considerable salary boost. There were over twenty applicants from the factory in question and just two of us from other factories in the group. In the event it was decided, under pressure from the chapel, that the appointment should come from inside the factory.

I then started to apply for jobs as composing room manager and, after a number of interviews which were unsatisfactory from various points of view I applied for a job at Martin

Cadbury at Prestbury, just outside Cheltenham. At the interview the director said "I think we've met before". He had visited Waterlow's to see the Linotype Elektrons in action and had remembered me. I was told the job was mine if I wanted it. I liked the look of the place, the family were happy to move there, so I accepted.

Then began a frantic search for a house. I wrote to all the estate agents in Cheltenham, made a short list of all the houses in the right price range and situated in the right areas, and one Saturday morning, after making appointments on the telephone, we set off on a viewing expedition. After an exhausting round of viewing we eventually found a nice three-bedroom detached house in Bishop's Cleeve. It was painted all the colours of the rainbow inside but the layout was good and there was a nice garden with open aspects, so we decided there and then that we would have it.

The annual dinner of the Foremen's Club took place a week or so before I left the company and when the chairman rose to make his speech I was with him in spirit and thankful that I was not going to have to make a speech that year. He finished, and sat down to applause. Then he stood up again and announced that he had a very pleasant duty to perform. He then called on me to go up to receive a presentation from my fellow managers so I had to make an impromptu speech after all. However, it was nice to leave the company on good terms with everybody.

One small aside to the annual dinner. At a prior committee meeting we were trying to decide on some entertainment to break up the dancing. John Driscoll, the chairman, said he had some contacts in the entertainment world and if we agreed we could leave it to him. At the next meeting he told us he had booked a group and an exotic dancer. We were all very naive in those days and I'm not sure what we expected from the dancer.

On the evening of the dinner, after the tables had been cleared away, we danced to the music of the group. Then the master of ceremonies asked us to take our seats and welcome the exotic dancer. Of course, she was a stripper, and a very good one too. She both looked and smelt nice but I think most of us were surprised and a little embarrassed when she started removing items of clothing and draping them around our necks. She concluded her act by attaching tassels to her nipples and twirling them round in time to the music, which particularly amused the female members of the party.

I put my foot in it by strolling over to the chairman's table and telling John's wife that the committee hadn't really wanted a stripper but that John had insisted. This to warning looks from John. He told me shortly afterwards that he was in the doghouse. His wife was apparently the only one in the room who was not amused.

Some weeks before I left Dunstable I was called in to see the works manager, Bob Baker, who asked me if I would take two visitors from our company in Belfast out to lunch as he was tied down with other matters. This I did and found them both very charming men. A week later I received a letter from one of them thanking me for my hospitality and extending the same to me if ever I found myself in Belfast.

A month or two later some friends came to visit me at Cheltenham and told me that the senior of these two "charming men" was in fact a hatchet man. Bob Baker had disappeared overnight and there had been massive redundancies throughout the factory. There was, however, some poetic justice. After the redundancies had been completed the hatchet man was himself dismissed.

Chapter 8

A short spell in the West Country

Martin Cadbury at Prestbury was part of the Martin Cadbury Group with factories at Cheltenham, Worcester, Salisbury, and Guildford. It was a fairly new but traditional printing company doing basically two jobs, origination and printing, with the binding and finishing being done at the Worcester factory. The sales force and estimators were based at Prestbury. The work was mainly promotional printing in the form of technical brochures and magazines of various types. I was in charge of half of the factory which used Monotype keyboards and casters for type composition. My colleague, Bob Thompson, a dour Scot, was in charge of the machine room which used Heidelberg flatbed printing machines, all of the same type, which meant in theory that at any time a job could be stopped and a new job put on to the machine with the minimum of inconvenience.

My first few days were spent in visiting the other factories in the group and getting to know the people in charge, those with whom I would have to liaise frequently in the course of my work. These were quite a busy and heady few days, after which reality took over.

I discovered that the morale of the men was low due to the fact that senior management had announced that the Christmas holidays were to start on Christmas Eve, in line with the other factories in the group and not the day before as had been hoped. The other factories were well-established plants and the work force was largely from people who had lived in the area all their lives, whereas many of those at the Prestbury plant had moved to Cheltenham from various parts of the country and they naturally wanted to get home in good time for the holiday. This decision had been made without any consultation with the chapel and understandably there was bad feeling. In the event, after some very heated discussions, the company had to reverse its decision. A little forethought could have saved a lot of grief which took weeks to smooth over.

On my first day at the factory, when I was being taken round by the factory manager, Mike Reeves, and introduced to the work force, I had noticed that the casting machines were still idle half an hour after work had commenced. One of the operators was a dyed-in-the-wool trade unionist who liked to quote rules and regulations, while his colleague was a local man who, although a good operator, was a little slow on the uptake. I pointed out to them that I expected the first machine to be in operation fifteen minutes after the commencement of work and the second ten minutes later. This was met with all sorts of fatuous arguments. "Well," I said, "other caster operatives in other factories throughout the country do this. Are you telling me that you are not up to their standard?" The following morning both machines were working on time.

One or two of the men tried it on at first, testing my knowledge I suppose. One man brought a job to me and asked how I would do it. "Don't you know how to do it?" I asked. "Yes," he replied. "Well why are you asking me then?" I said. On the whole, though, they were a good group and turned out a very high standard of work. Although I still represented management and was one "them" if ever a dispute arose, they soon accepted me as I tried to be scrupulously fair and took their side if I thought their cause was just.

The first month in particular was very difficult as I tried to get to grips with new systems, progress meetings, etc., and I was perpetually tired. One evening after work Bob and I were called to the company director's office. "You chaps think you are working very hard, and you are," he said, "but in three months' time I guarantee you'll be saying 'Hell, we had it easy back then'." And he was right. More and more work was given to us and we learned to cope with it and became much more efficient in the process.

There were one or two things with which I disagreed at Cadbury's, one of them being that the factory manager had this idea of uniformity throughout the works and wanted the two managers to wear white smocks and the men to wear blue smocks supplied by the company, all with the Martin Cadbury logo on the breast pocket, and to pay a few shillings a week for laundry. The idea of wearing a smock for a purely management position did not appeal to me and I refused to do so. A number of the men also refused to join the scheme, preferring to wear their choice of colour, be it khaki, grey or blue.

Shortly after I started work at Cadbury's, Mr. Ashcroft, the owner of the group, started an on-going course of management at their headquarters at Warminster. This was held once a month. The first meeting was for all managers but after that senior management and middle management meetings were held on different days. The course covered all aspects of management including production techniques, budgeting, balance sheets, etc., and was held in an old mill. Initially the format was a lively discussion in the morning on all aspects of management and production, followed by a pub lunch, and the serious work of budgeting, etc., in the afternoon.

This pub lunch was good in that it meant that we were able to meet and discuss things with our colleagues from other factories over a pint or two of bitter. The drawback to this was that in the afternoon, sitting in this lovely old mill with the sun filtering through the windows, one began to feel drowsy. I suggested to Mr. Ashcroft that it might be better if we did the serious work in the mornings when everyone was fresh and have the discussions in the afternoon when people's tongues were loosened by the odd pint. He agreed and thereafter the meetings were more successful.

Bob and I used to take it in turns to drive to Warminster. It was lovely to go out on a spring or summer morning and drive past the factory and out through the lovely Vale of Pewsey and forget the problems of work for the day. On one such occasion, Bob was driving, and suddenly the car lurched. We had a puncture. We stopped to change the wheel which was very dirty as the roads were wet and muddy and consequently our hands and wrists were filthy. We cleaned up as best we could and stopped further along the road at a garage to clean up in their washroom. Consequently when we arrived at Warminster the meeting had already started. Mr. Ashcroft said rather sarcastically "Good afternoon Bob, good afternoon Harry. Glad you could join us." "Did you never have a puncture Mr. Ashcroft?" Bob replied, in his broad Scots accent. Mr. Ashcroft was a very reasonable boss and he apologised to us both during coffee break. He was a man who would never overlook a possibility of making money. Behind the factory was a small triangle of land which was doing nothing. He planted Christmas trees on the plot which he said would bring in a few more pounds.

As it would be some weeks before we could move into our house at Bishop's Cleeve I had to go into lodgings. The company had found a place for me but it was far from satisfactory. It was in a three-bedroomed semi and I had the single room over the hallway. There was no central heating and the room was perpetually cold. I used to sleep wearing my socks for warmth. The landlady's idea of dinner, almost every evening, was sausage rolls, brussels sprouts and mashed potatoes, followed by peaches and custard. One day I was telling Eve, our accountant, about this. She said she had a friend who was looking for a paying guest and said she would recommend me to her.

I subsequently went to see Cathy, for that was the lady's name, who lived in a cottage at Hatherley. It was warm, cosy, and friendly. She asked me when I would like to move in. I said "How about tomorrow?" She said that would be fine. So I rapidly terminated my stay at my former lodgings on the feeble excuse that I was being sent away on a course and moved in with Cathy the following day. I had been told that she was a widow but I did not know then how recently she had been bereaved. I subsequently learned that it had been earlier that year and in consequence she was very unsure of herself. However, as time went by she began to regain her confidence. I did small DIY jobs for her to save her money, such as replacing broken handles on the drawers of the kitchen cabinet, fixing a hand rail on the stairs and unblocking the waste pipe from the shower unit.

On New Year's Eve I suggested that she might like to go for a seasonal drink at the pub just across the road. She hummed and hawed and eventually agreed. She went upstairs to get ready. Half an hour later she still hadn't come down. I called up to ask if she was alright and she came down in tears saying that she just couldn't face going out. I related this to Eve some days later and she invited me to visit her house that evening and meet her husband Ken and to bring Cathy with me. When

I got home from work I put this to her and once again she was very reluctant. "Let's just go across the road for a sherry," I said. "There won't be many people in there so early in the evening." She agreed to this and after we had had our sherries I suggested we go for a short walk, which was naturally in the direction of Eve's house. In due course we arrived at the house and were welcomed in. Cathy thoroughly enjoyed her evening and from then on she had little difficulty in going out and meeting people.

In the course of conversation she told Ken how much she enjoyed having me as a lodger. "He's unblocked my pipes and mended my drawers" she said. Ken gave me a broad wink. "Good for you, Harry," he said.

I was very well looked after at Cathy's until such time as the formalities were completed on my house at Bishop's Cleeve and I was able to resume a normal life once more.

As mentioned earlier, the house had been painted in all the colours of the rainbow inside, with blue ceilings, orange and magnolia walls with yellow inserts in the windows and various coloured paints. Fortunately the previous owner had left drums of emulsion paint in the garage, among them a large quantity of magnolia. Magnolia is not a bad neutral colour so I decided on a first aid treatment by painting all the woodwork white and all the walls magnolia. This worked very well and in a very short time the house was transformed. The blue ceiling in the sitting room had been painted over ordinary whitewash and peeled off in great sheets. This revealed hairline cracks in the plaster but was overcome by covering it with anaglypta paper and then using emulsion paint over that.

The previous owner had also warned me about the awful neighbours he had to one side and to the rear of the house. As it turned out they were very nice people with whom we became good friends. The bad apple had been the previous owner.

Bishop's Cleeve was quite a large village set below the towering mass of Cleeve Hill and looking towards the Malvern Hills on the other side of the valley, about 18 miles away, although if rain was threatening the hills would appear to be just a few fields away. The locals had a saying that if you could see the Malverns it was going to rain and if you couldn't see them it was raining. The people were very friendly. The doctor would stop and chat to you in the street and the manager at the local bank had turned down promotion so that he could remain at the branch. Some evenings he could be found at the Plough Inn at Prestbury, where he lived, not in the lounge but in the public bar with the locals. The village contained numerous houses owned by Smith's Industries who had planted flowering trees and shrubs along the wide verges which were maintained to a very high standard and in the Spring in particular it was a floral heaven. My drive to work at Prestbury, about two miles away, was through leafy lanes and was a good way to start the day.

Sometimes after a hard day's work coping with problems, some of which were not resolved at the end of the day, I would go home mentally exhausted but, living as we did below Cleeve Hill, which was 1,000 feet above sea level, I found that a good walk over the top was an excellent way to clear the mind and I'd return home completely refreshed, ready to cope with whatever the next day had to offer.

The Plough, at Prestbury, was a real old country pub with a thatched roof, flagstone floors, low beams, rustic furniture and a very large garden. We used to take the reps who came down from London to lunch there and they were fascinated. The landlord took orders from a hatchway in the public bar and then we would be served in the garden by one of several ladies who worked there. The beer they drank was called West Country Ale and they thought it was produced there. In fact it was made by one of the large breweries and the label was merely to create an illusion.

One of the smaller factories in the group, situated at Salisbury, was closed and some of the work and equipment, together with some of the personnel, were transferred to the Prestbury factory. Among the equipment were a number of type cases labelled Winsor and Newton. None of us had heard of a typeface by that name and it transpired that it was one of the narrow Grotesque faces which was used for printing the labels for Winsor and Newton paints.

One day I was told by one of the labourers that there were some men at the back door of the factory who wanted to buy some metal. They told me that they came from a fairground and that they wanted a quantity of lead to put around the bases of some of their machinery to hold it steady. I asked them how much they wanted and they said about half a ton. Scrap mono metal was at that time about £120 per ton and I said they could have half a ton at that price. They were clearly put out and said that it was only scrap and that it was worth nothing. I told them that was the price and they could either take it or leave it. They wandered off cursing and we made certain that all scrap metal was kept securely under lock and key after that.

Metal type was our largest single asset and twice a year work had to stop in the middle of the afternoon and all the metal in the type cases, together with all the scrap metal, had to be weighed. This went on well into the evening and again the following morning until the task was completed. This not only involved a large overtime bill but the loss of quite a number of hours of production time. I went into the cost of this operation, something which had not occurred to anyone to do before, and found that several tons of the metal would have to be stolen every six months to outweigh the cost of the weighing operation. After that it was stopped.

One morning I received a telephone call from the wife of the factory manager. He had been involved in a motoring accident the previous evening and although not seriously hurt he was badly bruised and shocked and would be off work for a few days. I was asked to take over his duties until he returned. This was a useful experience. At the time there was a national dispute in progress and I soon discovered why senior management appeared to have all the answers in their meetings with union officials. The Master Printers' Association appeared to have a more efficient communications system. I was informed by their secretary of the settlement of the dispute at least four hours before the F.O.C. requested a meeting to tell me about it.

Although this was only a temporary arrangement I soon discovered how much easier it was to give instructions when there was no face-to-face confrontation with the work force if any unpleasant decisions had to be made. This was the responsibility of the line manager.

I had been at Martin Cadbury's for about 21 months when I received a call from a man in London. He was starting a new printing company and needed a production manager. I had been recommended to him by Frank Glynn Jones, from IBM, and he seemed eager to obtain my services. The package I was offered was very good indeed, with a much higher salary, a personal insurance scheme, and a generous relocation allowance. After a couple of meetings with him in London I decided to accept his offer. Although my two years at Martin Cadbury's had been very exhilarating they had nevertheless been the hardest of my working life and I was anxious to move on.

I had to tender a month's notice and start an immediate search for a house somewhere near the main railway line to London. I eventually decided on Wolverton, now part of Milton Keynes, as the nearer one got to London the higher the prices of houses. We searched around, and because prices were higher at Wolverton than they were in the West Country we had to settle for a semi-detached chalet bungalow.

In due course the day came for my leaving. I invited all who wanted to to have a farewell drink with me at the local pub and forty of the staff turned up. By the time the last man had got his pint the first man had finished his and was ordering another round. They were all enjoying themselves so much that they forgot about the time and stayed until closing time at two-thirty, arriving back at work at about a quarter to three, much to the annoyance of Mike. I was glad that I did not have to go back to work that day, except to pick up my few remaining bits and pieces and to take my formal leave.

My younger son, Graham, had by this time reached the age of sixteen and had applied for and obtained employment at GCHQ headquarters which was just down the road from our factory. Our moving would mean that he would have to go into lodgings. One morning I awoke with the thought that perhaps he could be transferred to the Foreign and Commonwealth Office headquarters at Hanslope Park, where his brother worked. I 'phoned the personnel manager at GCHQ soon after I got to work and he agreed to see me later in the day. The outcome of the meeting was that, although personnel were not usually transferred, because Graham had not actually started work there he had spoken to his opposite number at Hanslope and, subject to a satisfactory interview, he could work there.

As a family we had been positively vetted so there was no problem there. On the Friday afternoon we took Graham to Hanslope for his formal interview and he was told to start there the following Monday morning. They had arranged hostel accommodation for him at Bletchley Park until such time as we moved to Wolverton and after that he could live at home. On the Sunday evening I drove him to Bletchley and saw him settled in his new accommodation. This was to be a tough few weeks for him, his first time away from home, but with his brother to turn to he quickly settled in.

It was at Bletchley Park that I experienced an example of "it's more than my job's worth". Traffic in and out of the Park is controlled by a barrier operated by a gatekeeper. I had seen Graham installed in his new quarters and stayed chatting with him for a while. Eventually I took my leave, turned the car round, and went back the way I had gone in, not noticing that there was a one-way system round the lake. There was no-one else about but when I reached the gate a pompous little man wearing a peaked cap came out of the gatehouse and would not raise the barrier until he had given me a lecture about the way to drive round the Park. I gave him a crocodile smile, said I was sorry, at the same time thinking unprintable things, and was eventually allowed to leave.

By the time I started work in London the factory was already under way and most of the staff had been engaged. It was hard going at first, involving working most evenings until about eight o'clock, but as I had lodgings in Finchley this did not matter and it also meant that I could leave in the middle of Friday afternoon to beat the rush hour traffic out of London and get back home to Bishop's Cleeve at a reasonable time.

The lodgings were with a lovely Irish lady who looked after me very well, probably too well. She also had a number of labourers who worked for Murphy's staying there and they had enormous appetites. I was given the same sized meals as they were and consequently began to put on weight. At the time I was there my father was extremely ill at Hertford and I was able to visit him. One evening I said I would be going to Hertford straight from work so I would not require a meal. When I arrived back at about 10.30 p.m. there was a full dinner keeping warm on the steamer. I felt obliged to eat it as she had been so kind.

At the factory a phototypesetting machine of a type of which I had no experience had been purchased and which I was expected to bring into operation. This posed a number of problems. In the first place it had been bought at an exhibition and was designed for a foreign market. In the second place it would not respond to the typed instructions given, and in the third place, although the marketing company was only a few miles away, they only had a few engineers who always seemed to be away somewhere.

Much of the work which had been taken on necessitated being set elsewhere and we relied heavily on their being able to deliver on time. One evening I received a telephone call from a customer who was a particularly nasty character and who used foul language in front of his office staff. He wanted a job that evening. I had staff working on it but it was physically impossible to deliver that evening. I told him he would receive the completed job first thing in the morning without fail. That was not good enough for him and he began to hurl vile abuse at me. Now it has never been in my nature to accept that from anyone and I told him so. He asked to be transferred to the managing director.

The following morning the M.D. asked me to see him in his office where he told me he thought that perhaps I was not the right man for the job and suggested that we should part company immediately with a generous severance payment. A month after I left the customer concerned became a director of the company. C'est la vie!

So, for the first time in my life I was out of work, an entirely new experience. Something had to be done immediately. I was already in the process of buying a house at Wolverton and I knew that McCorquodale Ltd. were situated there, so I went straight from London to Wolverton, presented myself at McCorquodale's and asked to see the personnel manager. He was good enough to see me without an appointment and asked me about myself and what I was looking for. When he learned that I had served my apprenticeship at Stephen Austin's he immediately warmed as he had been a production manager there some years previously. I said I did not necessarily want a management position and he told me there was a vacancy for a keyboard operator. He then introduced me to the branch secretary of the union who conveniently worked in the reading room and showed me over the factory.

There were three Monotype keyboards in a small room, together with a Linotype machine, and separated by a door from the casting room. It was a miniature hell on earth but I was assured that a new room was going to be built for the keyboards and on that assurance it was agreed that I start work there at the beginning of the following month. This would give me time to get my affairs in order and make the necessary arrangements for moving.

I drove back to Bishop's Cleeve to tell my wife that the bad news was that I had lost my job but the good news was that I had another one to go to. We were sorry to have to leave Bishop's Cleeve but the good thing was that the family would be together again for the first time in two years.

With my severance pay and a refund from the Inland Revenue I was actually better off than if I had been at work and was able to spend the next two weeks enjoying long walks on and around Cleeve Hill.

Chapter 9

Wolverton, and computer typesetting at last

At my interview it had been suggested that we might like to move into a company house until the purchase had been completed on our own house. Many of these houses had been previously owned by the railway works. Wolverton was a railway town and the houses were allocated according to one's status in the company. Senior management lived in large houses near to the works and the railway station while platelayers lived in small cottages in nearby New Bradwell, and there were various other grades in between. We were allocated an extremely large terraced house at the station end of the town. As this was only a temporary measure we could not furnish it as we would have liked, but it was reasonably comfortable.

We spent Christmas there but it was not one of our happy ones. Graham was home but was suffering from influenza and we had the worry that my father was dying. We visited him when we could and at my last visit, in February 1973, he had become very weak and said goodbye. Two days later my brother 'phoned to say that he had gone.

McCorquodale's was a long-established printing company with a very large factory and a large work force. I had expected quite a drop in income when I went there but they ran a bonus scheme and I quickly found that my standard of living didn't have to take too much of a plunge. The company were true to their word and a new keyboard room quickly took shape in a quiet area near one end of the composing room.

There were three of us in the room—Dick Birchall, George Bradburn, and me. We had ample working space, plenty of storage space and very good working conditions. To facilitate the flow of work I was asked to be chargehand and take responsibility for sorting out the work and for giving the apprentices training in basic keyboard operating. This worked very well as the other two were both very amenable chaps to work with.

Although this was a long way behind developments in the printing industry in general, the company made a tentative move towards cold typesetting. A second-hand Varitype machine was acquired and in due course a young lady arrived to train us on this piece of equipment. It was never going to be a success as the quality of output of the Varitype did not match up to the standards required. However, it did provide one or two diversions.

The young lady who was training us arrived one morning smelling very highly of perfume. It transpired that her boyfriend had given her a large bottle of Chanel No. 5 as a present which she had in her handbag. As she got out of her car she dropped the handbag and the bottle of perfume broke. She hung her coat and handbag on the coathook next to the one where George hung his. Consequently he arrived home for lunch smelling like a lady's boudoir. He had quite a lot of explaining to do to his wife!

We also experimented briefly with the Monotype electronic keyboard. I was sent on a course at the Monotype school in Redhill, which was extremely boring because the instructor, instead of showing me the differences between this keyboard and the old type, went right back to basic principles and I was confronted with a series of exercises normally used for beginners. I did, however, meet Don Brace, my old colleague from Stephen Austin's, who was working there.

Not long after I had been at McCorquodale's we had the annual chapel meeting and I was proposed as F.O.C. because of my previous management experience, the thinking being that I would know best how to deal with the current management. Although McCorquodale's didn't have photocomposition facilities it was an option they were looking into. There had been a long-standing dispute over the rate to be paid and the terms which the chapel sought were totally unrealistic. Shortly after I became F.O.C. a new personnel officer was appointed and, maybe because he wanted to make his mark, a new proposal was put on the table. The branch committee stated that this was the best offer in the area and that we should accept it. This was done and peace and harmony prevailed once more.

Much has been said in the past about the unions being too strong and trying to run the country and perhaps in some industries this was the case but in general the printing unions have always adopted a more moderate stance. It must not be forgotten that the management side also had its problem people, the empire builders. If as much effort had been put into production as into internal politics the whole of the industry would have been much more profitable and perhaps more ready to cope with technological changes.

Of course, we had our share of trouble-makers. On two occasions I had to defend a man, an inveterate liar, who was guilty of a misdemeanour and who was patently in the wrong. I knew it, he knew it, and the managing director and personnel officer both knew it. It went against my better judgement but as his union representative I had to argue his case. On the second occasion he was brought before the chapel committee when he was warned that if he ever stepped out of line again he would be reported to the branch committee for bringing the union into disrepute.

There was a new F.O.C. in the machine chapel and we suggested to the personnel officer that we should attend an F.O.C.s training course. He agreed to this and we spent a very intensive and informative week at Rewley House, the external students' accommodation at Oxford. There were excellent guest speakers and the food and accommodation was of a very high standard, but the most rewarding part of the course was the companionship and mutual under-standing between union members from all parts of the country and from the national executive members. We worked hard throughout the day and in the evening, after we had visited one of the many hostelries in the town, we gathered together in the basement for further discussions, usually till midnight. It was suggested at the end of the course that the name of the house be changed to "Unruly House".

I recall one amusing incident. One of the men had come by car and because of the parking regulations had to move it from time to time to a different place. One day we had a visiting speaker, a don from one of the colleges. He was a Welshman with a wry sense of humour. We told him that one of our colleagues may be a little late because he had to move his car. When John arrived at the meeting he said: "I apologise for being late but due to circumstances entirely beyond my control I was unavoidably delayed." "Oh," replied the don, "I though perhaps you were the chap who had to move his car."

About this time the deputy composing room foreman retired and it was my job to arrange his retirement party. This took place at the Barge Inn at Woolstone. We were allocated a raised area to ourselves and the evening was a great success. I was invited by the works manager to apply for the vacant position. I did so but this caused such a commotion within the chapel committee that for the first time in my life I backed down and withdrew my application. George applied and was successful, leaving just Dick and me to operate the keyboards.

It was some time during this period that I had one of my memorable experiences in the printing industry. We were on holiday in Germany and spent a day in Mainz. My wife and daughter went to look round the shops while I visited the Gutenberg Museum. There, among other things, I saw the original Gutenberg bible. Johann Gutenberg invented moveable type, making the printing of books a much speedier process and thus making them available to many more people. He was not popular with the clergy for doing so because it robbed them of some of their power but it was the beginning of a revolution in the field of education and learning. It was arguably the most far-reaching revolution in world history.

I have previously mentioned the ceremonies which took place when an apprentice came out of his time. At Bletchley it was the practice to smother the apprentice in printing ink and tie him to a lamppost in the town centre and leave him there. That was bad enough but at McCorquodale's it was verging on the barbaric. As before, the junior apprentices were allowed to use the morning decorating a forme trolley. At lunch time the apprentice concerned was taken to the local and, after he had had a few drinks, was made to drink a yard of ale. Consequently he arrived back at work considerably the worse for wear. He was then placed in the truck and wheeled round the various departments where all manner of things were poured over him—printing ink, chads, chicken manure, and, an innovation from the casting room, warm treacle down the inside of his trousers. Usually the hapless lad would be taken home wrapped in plastic sheeting and left to clean himself up. Each year new refinements were sought until at last things went too far. One boy had oily swarf poured over him which was a serious danger to health and one of the men trod in a lump of old printing ink and unwittingly carried it home on his shoe and ruined his carpet. It was decided by management, quite wisely, not to allow this practice in future.

Eventually we were informed that the hot metal side, i.e. the Monotype keyboards and casters, would be disposed of and the Linotronic VIP system was going to be installed in its place. A new room was to be built for it at the far end of the factory, together with a new composing room. However, there would inevitably be redundancies. A number of people would have to be retrained for the new system and more keyboard operators would be needed, together with a copy preparer. For this last position a number of us were given a test, similar to those used to select computer programmers, which involved working out a series of flow charts with various alternatives. I came out on top and was selected to be copy preparer.

Together with Terry Jeary, the foreman, I was sent to Cheltenham on a two-week course to learn all about the system. We turned up on the Monday morning of the first week to be greeted by the instructor, Chris McBride, who had been one of my keyboard operators at Martin Cadbury's. Another young man on the course, Steve, training to be a salesman of the system, was previously one of my apprentices from the same firm. It was a very intensive two weeks but I felt that we were finally moving out of hot metal and into the future of printing.

The VIP keyboards had small screens with, I think, eleven lines of text, some of them status lines, i.e. typeface, size, measure, etc. and gave a limited means of correction. They produced a paper tape which was taken to the photosetter for processing. The photosetter utilised strips of film which were clipped to a tower which rotated at high speed round a flashing light source to produce the image. Each film strip carried one fount of type. The film cassette was then taken to the developer to produce a bromide for the reader to check for errors. Any errors had to be typeset in small blocks and pasted over the original.

As is usual with any new system some of the compositors took to it like ducks to water but there were inevitably one or two whose minds could not adequately grasp a new concept and who continued to think of how things were done using hot metal. This was to be their eventual downfall as there was soon another round of redundancies, which included Terry the foreman, and George took over his job.

One day George announced that he was going to emigrate to Australia, leaving the foreman's job vacant. This was a month or so before the four-yearly IPEX exhibition, which that year was being held at the National Exhibition Centre at Birmingham. This time I applied for the vacancy and was successful. I was told to go to IPEX with a view to future developments in photo-composition and computer type-setting. I spent two separate days at the exhibition. On the first day it was a general look round to see what was on offer. I was impressed by one particular system and on the second day spent a long time having an in-depth look at it and weighing up its possibilities.

Shortly after George departed. He had laid on snacks at one of the local pubs and we adjourned there at lunchtime where I presented him with a clock on behalf of the department. After that I bought everyone a pint and I became foreman.

I was not happy with the quality of some of the film strips and sought to rectify the situation. By a strange quirk in the scheme of things Linotype and Machinery Ltd., the makers of the VIP system, had allowed my old boss Mr. Stanley Harrison, then retired, to make these film strips. I made an appointment to see him and it was strange in some respects that I was now telling him what I wanted done. But Mr.

Harrison is, and always was, a true gentleman, and we had a very comfortable association during the life of the VIP system.

While the VIP system was doing a fairly adequate job things were moving quickly in the area of computer type-setting and the company, very much aware of the intense competition in the printing industry, didn't want to be left behind. Nevertheless, a new system would be a very large investment so I was given the brief to look at all possible systems and evaluate their potential and capabilities. I made a very stringent list of requirements such as tabulation, text rotation, ease of operation, availability, costs, etc.

Then began a series of visits to various companies, usually in the company of Howard Mordue, our technical manager. We were treated like royalty wherever we went because every manufacturer was intent on creating a market for its own equipment. Many were destined to fall by the way. Some of the systems investigated, although of excellent quality, failed to meet our strict criteria and we eventually finished up with two possibles. They both had their pluses and minuses and with each visit we made to them they had made further improvements, sometimes one having the advantage and sometimes the other. Eventually we went to a computer typesetting exhibition at Brighton and one of the companies, Pagitek, which had attracted my attention at IPEX, had suddenly got its act completely together and had come up with an excellent compact system which met all our requirements.

Gone were the keyboards and all the separate bits and pieces which had typified the earlier models. Now there was just a computer with its keyboard which fed straight into a laser printer or the photo unit. From keyboard to camera-ready copy at the touch of a button. This was the one we decided to recommend.

Ted Pankhurst, our personnel manager, decided that I, together with Stuart, a newly appointed deputy machine room supervisor, should go on the NEBS course at Watford college as all supervisors had been sent there in the past. This meant travelling to Watford one day a week for a year and it was one of the most boring experiences of my printing life.

So much time was wasted. This course was for supervisors from all walks of life, few of them involved with production problems, and the tutors were academics with plenty of theoretical experience but not much of the hurly-burly of factory life. The evening instructor, for example, had been giving the course for many years and we gathered from supervisors who had attended the course previously that he was still using exactly the same examples as he had used for them. In spite of this he continued to write out his overhead projection sheets there and then instead of having them all nicely prepared.

There were two courses running in parallel. Our group dealt with working conditions, spatial relations, interviewing techniques, etc. in the afternoon, and balance sheets, flow charts, etc. in the evening, while with the other group the roles were reversed. In the middle of the course there was a weekend session at a conference hotel at Bournemouth when both groups came together. This began on Friday evening and continued till Sunday lunchtime. The weekend allowed us to meet socially and the bar was open into the small hours.

After a long session on the Saturday afternoon one of the ladies on the course, Shirley, whose room was next to mine, said that she was dying for a cup of tea but she only had a tea maker in her room with which she was having difficulties. I had a kettle in my room and suggested that after we had showered and changed she should come in for a cup of tea. This she did and we chatted about families and general things. As she left my room another man, also on the course, came out of his room, which was the other side of mine. He gave me a knowing look but said nothing.

That evening in the bar it was getting late and the subject of conversation turned to politics. Knowing that we had probably been talked about I turned to Shirley and said "I think I'm going to turn in. Are you coming?" "Yes" she replied, and we left together, having a good laugh as we made our ways to our respective rooms.

I had been on specific management courses in the past, from line management to middle management, although none of them had been certificated. However, at the end of the year we sat the exam. I gave them the answers they wanted, although I disagreed with many of them, and duly received my certificate.

Over the course of the year every student had to produce a project which was a practical solution to a problem in his or her company. This would have to be typed, set out in a logical and easily understandable form, and presented suitably bound. For my project I set out the reasons why McCorquodale's should have the Pagitek system, with the costs and savings involved, this being a system which I had come to know well over the previous four years.

Some time after the end of the course a new director joined the company. He was high on enthusiasm and wanted to see for himself the kind of equipment we were interested in. Once again the visits began, including one or two which Howard and I had already ruled out. Eventually, however, he agreed that we had made the best choice and once again it was put on hold.

Shortly after this a new managing director was appointed who, it was stated, was going to make McCorquodale's a family firm. What in actual fact happened was another round of redundancies. I was called to the M.D.'s office and told that the company was buying the Pagitek system and that the composing department and the plate making department were being merged. I was under no illusions about my future with regard to the new department as I had only two years to go until retirement, whereas the foreman of the platemaking department was a much younger man, albeit with little knowledge of composition. I was given the choice of taking redundancy or staying to operate the equipment which I had chosen over the previous four years. I chose to stay, partly because of the effect it would have on my pension when I retired in two years' time, and partly because I knew the system better than anyone else and therefore nobody would be able to tell me how to do my job.

We had to attend a course on the Pagitek system which could be in either London or Tewkesbury. I chose to go to Tewkesbury, partly because I could get there just as easily as I could get to London and it was a more pleasant journey, and partly because I had met the instructor at IPEX and was impressed with his style of teaching. Three of us operated the system, which was soon turning out work at a much faster rate than previously. Some jobs which had previously taken three days to turn round were now being sent out on proof the same day as they were received. My choice of equipment had been proved to be the right one.

In addition to the redundancies it was decided to sell the factory, which occupied a premium site in Wolverton, and relocate into part of the envelope factory on the other side of the road. This would now become a small, compact factory, and would be known as McCorquodale Confidential Print.

The new factory consisted basically of two large rooms, both open plan. In one were the origination sections—composing, reading and platemaking—and in the other were the printing machines and the binding and finishing departments. Working conditions were good although there was no natural light.

Although I was once again working with men of whom I had previously been in charge things worked out very well and I plodded along happily until my retirement.

The day before my sixty-fifth birthday I went in to work as usual and worked until about mid-day. I was then taken out to lunch and had the rest of the afternoon off. The following morning I took in drinks and snacks and set up a bar in the darkroom. Throughout the morning people drifted in from all over the factory to wish me luck and at lunch time there was a meeting in the department where I was presented with a power drill from the work force and a wristwatch from the directors. After fifty-one years at work I was at last a free man. That appears to imply that I had been serving a sentence. Not a bit of it. Although there were ups and downs in my working life, there were more ups than downs. I enjoyed being a printer and mixing with printers.

Chapter 10

What of the future?

With the advent of desktop publishing systems everyone became a printer overnight with sometimes disastrous results. Few of the people using these machines had a printing background and knew little or nothing of printing conventions. Many of those using this new technology were brought up in offices using conventional typewriters with restraints imposed by mechanical limitations. Em rules, en rules and hyphens were all the same to them. Leaders were confused with ellipses and any resemblance of style was completely ignored. There was overuse of borders and clipart and with hundreds of typefaces at their fingertips many small publications resembled type catalogues. This has, however, made a considerable impact on small print shops. More and more work is being done by fewer and fewer people and one can only wonder what changes will take place in the next fifty years, given the rate of acceleration in printing technology.

The whole scene has changed from the early days of my apprenticeship, much of it over the last few years. What was once a strictly male preserve, largely because of the intense physical effort involved, now has more and more women employed and, it has to be said, for some of the tasks where neatness and creativity is involved, they are eminently more suitable than men.

Over two thousand years ago Virgil, the great Roman poet, said "Non omnia possumus omnes" which translated means "We can't all do everything". There is now equipment in operation where a job can be set up, made up in full colour, and sent to the printing machine at the touch of a button with no one else involved but a single operator.

However, all is not gloom and doom. Somebody asked me if I thought that the computer would eventually take over from books. The short answer is "no". You can't curl up in bed with a good computer; you can't take a computer with you for in-flight reading; nor is it convenient to take a computer to a shady spot in the garden or country for a quiet read; and it is absolutely useless for propping up a wonky table leg. The computer is excellent for a work of reference. Just log on to the Internet or insert a CD ROM, type in the subject you are looking for and, hey presto, there is the answer on the screen before you. But then what do you do? You print it out to read it.

There will always be the need for the printed word and while there is that need so will there be the need for skilled printers to present the printed word in an easy-to-read attractive format. Perhaps in fifty years' time someone else will write a book about their lifetime in print. I would like to think that I would still be around to read it!

Books Published by THE BOOK CASTLE

CHANGES IN OUR LANDSCAPE: Aspects of Bedfordshire, Buckinghamshire and the Chilterns 1947-1992: Eric Meadows. Over 350 photographs from the author's collection spanning nearly 50 years.

COUNTRYSIDE CYCLING IN BEDFORDSHIRE, BUCKINGHAMSHIRE AND HERTFORDSHIRE: Mick Payne. Twenty rides on and off-road for all the family.

PUB WALKS FROM COUNTRY STATIONS: Bedfordshire and Hertfordshire: Clive Higgs. Fourteen circular country rambles, each starting and finishing at a railway station and incorporating a pub stop at a mid way point.

PUB WALKS FROM COUNTRY STATIONS: Buckinghamshire and Oxfordshire: Clive Higgs. Circular rambles incorporating pub-stops.

LOCAL WALKS: South Bedfordshire and North Chilterns: Vaughan Basham. Twenty-seven thematic circular walks.

LOCAL WALKS: North and Mid Bedfordshire: Vaughan Basham. Twenty-five thematic circular walks.

FAMILY WALKS: Chilterns South: Nick Moon. Thirty 3 to 5 mile circular walks.

FAMILY WALKS: Chilterns North: Nick Moon. Thirty shorter circular walks.

CHILTERN WALKS: Hertfordshire, Bedfordshire and North Bucks: Nick Moon.

CHILTERN WALKS: Buckinghamshire: Nick Moon.

CHILTERN WALKS: Oxfordshire and West Buckinghamshire: Nick Moon. A trilogy of circular walks, in association with the Chiltern Society. Each volume contains 30 circular walks.

OXFORDSHIRE WALKS: Oxford, the Cotswolds and the Cherwell Valley: Nick Moon.

OXFORDSHIRE WALKS: Oxford, the Downs and the Thames Valley: Nick Moon. Two volumes that complement Chiltern Walks: Oxfordshire, and complete coverage of the county, in association with the Oxford Fieldpaths Society. Thirty circular walks in each.

THE D'ARCY DALTON WAY: Nick Moon. Long-distance footpath across the Oxfordshire Cotswolds and Thames Valley, with various circular walk suggestions.

THE CHILTERN WAY: Nick Moon. A guide to the new 133 mile circular Long-Distance Path through Bedfordshire, Buckinghamshire, Hertfordshire and Oxfordshire, as planned by the Chiltern Society.

JOURNEYS INTO BEDFORDSHIRE: Anthony Mackay. Foreword by The Marquess of Tavistock, Woburn Abbey. A lavish book of over 150 evocative ink drawings.

COCKNEY KID & COUNTRYMEN: Ted Enever. The Second World War remembered by the children of Woburn Sands and Aspley Guise. A six year old boy is evacuated from London's East End to start life in a Buckinghamshire village.

JOURNEYS INTO BUCKINGHAMSHIRE: Anthony Mackay. Superb line drawings plus background text: large format landscape gift book.

BUCKINGHAMSHIRE MURDERS: Len Woodley. Nearly two centuries of nasty crimes.

WINGRAVE: A Rothschild Village in the Vale: Margaret and Ken Morley. Thoroughly researched and copiously illustrated survey of the last 200 years in this lovely village between Aylesbury and Leighton Buzzard.

HISTORIC FIGURES IN THE BUCKINGHAMSHIRE LANDSCAPE: John Houghton. Major personalities and events that have shaped the county's past, including Bletchley Park.

TWICE UPON A TIME: John Houghton. North Bucks short stories loosely based on fact.

SANCTITY AND SCANDAL IN BEDS AND BUCKS: John Houghton. A miscellany of unholy people and events.

MANORS and MAYHEM, PAUPERS and PARSONS: Tales from Four Shires: Beds., Bucks., Herts. and Northants: John Houghton. Little known historical snippets and stories.

FOLK: Characters and Events in the History of Bedfordshire and Northamptonshire: Vivienne Evans. Anthology of people of yesteryear -arranged alphabetically by village or town.

JOHN BUNYAN: His Life and Times: Vivienne Evans. Highly praised and readable account.

THE RAILWAY AGE IN BEDFORDSHIRE: Fred Cockman. Classic, illustrated account of early railway history.

A LASTING IMPRESSION: Michael Dundrow. A boyhood evacuee recalls his years in the Chiltern village of Totternhoe near Dunstable.

GLEANINGS REVISITED: Nostalgic Thoughts of a Bedfordshire Farmer's Boy: E.W. O'Dell. His own sketches and early photographs adorn this lively account of rural Bedfordshire in days gone by.

BEDFORDSHIRE'S YESTERYEARS Vol 2: The Rural Scene: Brenda Fraser-Newstead. Vivid first-hand accounts of country life two or three generations ago.

BEDFORDSHIRE'S YESTERYEARS Vol 3: Craftsmen and Tradespeople: Brenda Fraser-Newstead. Fascinating recollections over several generations practising many vanishing crafts and trades.

BEDFORDSHIRE'S YESTERYEARS Vol 4: War Times and Civil Matters: Brenda Fraser-Newstead. Two World Wars, plus transport, law and order, etc.

PROUD HERITAGE: A Brief History of Dunstable, 1000-2000AD: Vivienne Evans. Century by century account of the town's rich tradition and key events, many of national significance.

DUNSTABLE WITH THE PRIORY: 1100-1550: Vivienne Evans. Dramatic growth of Henry I's important new town around a major crossroads.

DUNSTABLE IN TRANSITION: 1550-1700: Vivienne Evans. Wealth of original material as the town evolves without the Priory.

DUNSTABLE DECADE: THE EIGHTIES: A Collection of Photographs: Pat Lovering. A souvenir book of nearly 300 pictures of people and events in the 1980s.

STREETS AHEAD: An Illustrated Guide to the Origins of Dunstable's Street Names: Richard Walden. Fascinating text and captions to hundreds of photographs, past and present, throughout the town.

DUNSTABLE IN DETAIL: Nigel Benson. A hundred of the town's buildings and features, plus town trail map.

OLD DUNSTABLE: Bill Twaddle. A new edition of this collection of early photographs.

BOURNE and BRED: A Dunstable Boyhood Between the Wars: Colin Bourne. An elegantly written, well illustrated book capturing the spirit of the town over fifty years ago.

OLD HOUGHTON: Pat Lovering. Pictorial record capturing the changing appearances of Houghton Regis over the past 100 years.

ROYAL HOUGHTON: Pat Lovering. Illustrated history of Houghton Regis from the earliest of times to the present.

THE STOPSLEY BOOK: James Dyer. Definitive, detailed account of this historic area of Luton. 150 rare photographs.

THE STOPSLEY PICTURE BOOK: James Dyer. New material and photographs make an ideal companion to The Stopsley Book.

PUBS and PINTS: The Story of Luton's Public Houses and Breweries: Stuart Smith. The background to beer in the town, plus hundreds of photographs, old and new.

LUTON AT WAR I: As compiled by the Luton News in 1947, a well illustrated thematic account.

THE CHANGING FACE OF LUTON: An Illustrated History: Stephen Bunker, Robin Holgate and Marian Nichols. Luton's development from earliest times to the present busy industrial town. Illustrated in colour and mono.

WHERE THEY BURNT THE TOWN HALL DOWN: Luton, The First World War and the Peace Day Riots, July 1919: Dave Craddock. Detailed analysis of a notorious incident.

THE MEN WHO WORE STRAW HELMETS: Policing Luton,
1840-1974: Tom Madigan. Fine chronicled history, many rare photographs; author~served in Luton Police for fifty years.

BETWEEN THE HILLS: The Story of Lilley, a Chiltern Village: Roy Pinnock. A priceless piece of our heritage - the rural beauty remains but the customs and way of life described here have largely disappeared.

KENILWORTH SUNSET: A Luton Town Supporter's Journal:
Tim Kingston. Frank and funny account of football's ups and downs.

A HATTER GOES MAD!: Kristina Howells. Luton Town footballers, officials and supporters talk to a female fan.

LEGACIES: Tales and Legends of Luton and the North Chilterns:
Vic Lea. Mysteries and stories based on fact, including Luton Town Football Club. Many photographs.

THREADS OF TIME: Shela Porter. The life of a remarkable mother and businesswoman, spanning the entire century and based in Hitchin and (mainly) Bedford.

LEAFING THROUGH LITERATURE: Writers' Lives in Herts and Beds: David Carroll. Illustrated short biographies of many famous authors and their connections with these counties.

A PILGRIMAGE IN HERTFORDSHIRE: H.M. Alderman. Classic, between-the-wars tour round the county, embellished with line drawings.

THE VALE OF THE NIGHTINGALE: Molly Andrews. Several generations of a family, lived against a Harpenden backdrop.

SUGAR MICE AND STICKLEBACKS: Childhood Memories of a Hertfordshire Lad: Harry Edwards. Vivid evocation of gentle pre-war in an archetypal village, Hertingfordbury.

SWANS IN MY KITCHEN: Lis Dorer. Story of a Swan Sanctuary near Hemel Hempstead.

THE HILL OF THE MARTYR: An Architectural History of St.Albans Abbey:
Eileen Roberts. Scholarly and readable chronological narrative history of Hertfordshire and Bedfordshire's famous cathedral. Fully illustrated with photographs and plans.

CHILTERN ARCHAEOLOGY: RECENT WORK: A Handbook for the Next Decade: edited by Robin Holgate. The latest views, results and excavations by twenty-three leading archaeologists throughout the Chilterns.

THE TALL HITCHIN INSPECTOR'S CASEBOOK: A Victorian Crime Novel Based on Fact: Edgar Newman. Worthies of the time encounter more archetypal villains.

SPECIALLY FOR CHILDREN

VILLA BELOW THE KNOLLS: A Story of Roman Britain: Michael Dundrow. An exciting adventure for young John in Totternhoe and Dunstable two thousand years ago.

THE RAVENS: One Boy Against the Might of Rome: James Dyer. On the Barton Hills and in the south-east of England as the men of the great fort of Ravensburgh (near Hexton) confront the invaders.

THE BOOK CASTLE, 12 Church Street, Dunstable,
Bedfordshire LU5 4RU
Tel: (01582) 605670 Fax (01582) 662431
Email: bc@book-castle.co.uk

SUGAR MICE AND STICKLEBACKS
by Harry Edwards

Memories of a typical English village, Hertingfordbury, in the pre-war days when life was slower and gentler.... When the grocer, baker, cobbler, tailor, post-office, sweet-shop and builder's yard were all close at hand; the milk was delivered in a horse drawn cart. Facilities included a village school, a branch-line railway station, a Memorial Hall, a cricket pitch and pavilion, and the imposing Church of St. Mary with its Old Rectory. A vivid picture of country life is conjured up. Harry Edwards was born in a cottage next to the mill, and enjoyed a close family life. The luxuries of his mother's home-made cakes and pastries, his father's home grown produce, the early impact of radio and eventually main sewerage! The occasional spectacular flying displays nearby were a welcome diversion, as were visits to the village by Cycling Touring Club groups of fifty or so people, resplendent in their plus-fours. Boyhood pleasures only needed a simple stick or ball; hours of fun could be found just in sorting out mother's button tin; or a more ambitious project could lead to a rickety trolley or punt. A special joy to Harry as a youngster was splashing about with the gang in the endlessly fascinating river - or fishing by jar for sticklebacks in the extensive watercress beds.

A Book Castle Publication

COCKNEY KID AND COUNTRYMEN

The Second World War remembered by the children of Woburn Sands and Aspley Guise

by Ted Enever

On the evening of Saturday 7th September 1940, London's East End lay under a pall of smoke from heavy bombing by the German Luftwaffe. It was the beginning of what history was to record as the Blitz. Six year old Ted and his parents were victims of that first attack. With home and possessions lost, they left London to find safety, shelter and a new way of life in the villages of Woburn Sands and Aspley Guise. "Cockney Kid and Countrymen" is Ted Enever's story of that new way of life and a snapshot of the wartime years vividly remembered by the village children of the time.

Ted was educated at Bedford Modern School and entered journalism in 1951 with the Bletchley District Gazette. After two years national service he continued his career as a freelance journalist, with various large organisations. On retirement he was working for Milton Keynes Development Corporation. A founder member of the Bletchley Park Trust and now a Patron, Ted is author of "Britain's Best Kept Secret - Ultra's base at Bletchley Park."

A Book Castle Publication

A LASTING IMPRESSION
by Michael Dundrow

Michael Dundrow experienced an event in his formative years which strongly coloured or even completely changed the rest of his life.

This book describes one boy's overwhelming experience - wartime evacuation - which has left a truly lasting impression on his adult life. For this twelve year old from London's East End, to be dumped among a family of strangers on a large and busy farm below the Chilterns in Bedfordshire was a make or break experience of the first order.

Enriched by his years on the farm and in the village of Totternhoe, the adventures with new found friends, the sheer interest, fun and hard work of farm life and also the sowing of the seeds of appreciation of that lovely corner of South Bedfordshire, the details are all here, written with great affection. Although written fifty years after these unforgettable things happened, the story is undimmed by the passage of time.

In this evocative picture of wartime England are many glimpses of a way of village and farm life that has altered so dramatically in recent years as to be almost unrecognisable today.

A Book Castle Publication

THREADS OF TIME
by Shela Porter

A pale-faced city child is evacuated from London during the Zeppelin raids of 1917. In Hitchin she takes a dressmaking apprenticeship and opens her own workshop with customers including the local gentry and the young Flora Robson. Moving to Bedford on her marriage, her sewing skills help her rapidly growing family to survive the Depression; working long hours during the exigencies of war-time Britain, it is her re-designed battle-jacket that Glenn Miller is wearing when he disappears over the Channel in 1944, and entertainers Bing Crosby and Bob Hope leave comics and candy for her 'cute kids'. For five years after the war the family run a small cafe in the town but sewing then sees her through again as the business is sold, she is widowed with a nine-year-old son to raise, all her children gradually leave and she moves away to be wardrobe mistress to a big operatic society in High Wycombe. Finally she settles in a small cottage opposite the great airship sheds at Cardington from where she once watched the ill-fated R101 take off on its last journey in 1930. A mirror of her times, this gripping biography tells the story of a remarkable lady, a talented dressmaker, mostly in Hitchin and Bedford - played out against the unfolding drama of the entire twentieth century.

A Book Castle Publication

A PILGRIMAGE IN HERTFORDSHIRE

H.M. Alderman

A PILGRIMAGE INTO HERTFORDSHIRE
by H.M.Alderman

How well do you know the Hertfordshire of today?

How much has it changed over the course of a lifetime?

This classic account of the county offers a guided tour round the Hertfordshire of 1930. Many of the best-known landmarks, described and illustrated here, still stand - some, sadly, are lost.

Hertfordshire between the wars was certainly less populous, much quieter in every way. But the essential character of its busy market towns, peaceful villages and lovely countryside is recognisable from these pen pictures of yesteryear as the Hertfordshire of today.

Measure the parts of the county you know best against these evocative descriptions from a bygone age.

A Book Castle Publication

JOURNEYS INTO BEDFORDSHIRE
AND
JOURNEYS INTO BUCKINGHAMSHIRE
by Anthony Mackay

These two books of ink drawings reveal an intriguing historic heritage and capture the spirit of England's rural heartland, ranging widely over cottages and stately homes, over bridges, churches and mills, over sandy woods, chalk downs and watery river valleys.

Every corner of Bedfordshire and Buckinghamshire has been explored in the search for material, and, although the choice of subjects is essentially a personal one, the resulting collection represents a unique record of the environment today. The notes and maps, which accompany the drawings, lend depth to the books, and will assist others on their own journeys around the counties. Anthony Mackay's pen-and-ink drawings are of outstanding quality. An architectural graduate, he is equally at home depicting landscapes and buildings. The medium he uses is better able to show both depth and detail than any photograph.

A Book Castle Publication